to woody with love
from Marlene.

Be still & listen to
God as you read This!

He Called Me Rhea

Rhea Zakich

Dedicated to all those who taught me so much.

Contents

Introduction

Introduction

People have difficulty finding each other and relating to each other, one of the reasons being that we speak different languages within the English language. For some of us, our primary language is Head Talk, while for others it's Heart Talk. If we're not aware of what language we're speaking and what language the other person is speaking, we don't really understand each other and we don't connect.

One of my intentions for writing this book is to help people recognize both of these languages, so they can relate to each other in the same language.

I also desire for readers to learn about healing hidden wounds and how to gain freedom from pain, both physical and emotional.

This book is my spiritual autobiography, but I pray it will be much more than that for you, the reader. I pray that each of you will develop a more intimate relationship with Christ.

"Lord, make my spiritual journey a teaching and learning tool that can enhance the lives of those who are seeking more meaningful relationships and deliverance from past hurts. May I always give you the glory. Amen"

Chapter 1

Is This All There Is?

By the time I was thirty years old, I had fulfilled all the dreams I had as a young girl. In my teen-age years, I thought that the ultimate goal was to be married to a nice handsome man who made good money. I would live in an attractive house in a desirable neighborhood and have lots of friends. Owning two cars was almost unheard of in those days, so I thought my dream of having two cars was really far out.

On the night of my thirtieth birthday in 1965, I suddenly realized all my dreams had been fulfilled. I had attained every goal I had set for myself. But, instead of feeling a sense of accomplishment I felt empty. *Is this all there is?* I wondered. I felt no excitement or joy at having "arrived."

Up to this point in my life, I had prided myself on being a fantastic mother. I kept the house neat and clean, and things ran smoothly. My two sons, Darin and Dean, were preschoolers, and I spent my days with them meeting their needs. I thought the best mother in the world was one who took her children to the doctor for their checkups, gave them vitamins, read them bedtime stories, pulled them in a red wagon, put color-coordinated clothes on them, and sang to them. I was even able to anticipate things happening and take proper action before they occurred. That's what I thought every mother should strive for.

But on the eve of my birthday, a light went on and it didn't come from the candles on my birthday cake. Everything in my life was predictable. There were no highs. There were no lows. Everything remained the same... day after day. *Boring.*

Of course, I couldn't tell anyone I felt bored because I was always *doing something*. I was active in my church: choir, Sunday school, committees, and women's group. I had been in a prayer group which seemed to meet my needs, at least up until that point.

1

I drove my boys to nursery school on alternate days of the week. So, how could I be bored?

As I lay in bed, a startling thought occurred to me. *If I live to age sixty, my life is half over!* What had I done? What difference did it make to anyone that I had lived? Oh yes, I'd given birth to two babies, but that's wasn't so unusual. I felt insignificant, as if I was missing something. *Do other women feel this way?*

Eventually, I fell asleep, not realizing that my questions had opened the door to answers. My life was about to change, though I didn't know it.

~

I wasn't always involved in church activities. As a child, I had never stepped inside a church for a wedding, funeral, or any other event. My first exposure to church was when I was twenty-four years old.

When my babies were one and two years old, something I looked forward to each day was taking a coffee break with Alice, my next door neighbor. But she was never available on Sunday. I would see her taking her three little boys somewhere in the car. When I asked her where she went every Sunday morning, she said she and the children went to church. I didn't want her to know that I'd never gone to church and didn't know what they did there.

I asked her what she liked about church. When she said, "I put the kids in the nursery and go to the sanctuary…" Before she could finish her sentence, I said, "Can I go?" I had never left the boys with anyone and had no idea what a sanctuary was, but it sounded like some kind of haven and I was desperate for a break from mothering.

The next Sunday I went with Alice, having no idea what I was getting myself into (it could have been a communist party meeting for all I knew, but it didn't matter to me).

The nursery was in a small cottage next to a big Spanish-looking building. My children were welcomed and taken by the attendants to where the toys were.

Then the scary part came. Alice led me to the big doors that led into the church. I didn't know what to expect, but a man in a suit took us to a place to sit about six rows back from the stage. The room was full of serious-looking people all facing the front. I felt like they were all looking at me. No one else was talking, so I didn't ask any questions. The man handed each of us what looked like a menu. I glanced around to see if I was supposed to look at it. When I did open it, I didn't recognize some of the strange words like *Prelude, Introit, Doxology, Offertory, Lectionary, Sermon,* and *Benediction.*

I don't remember much of what was said since I was more concerned with knowing what to do. When certain organ music started playing, everyone knew to stand. But by the time I got my long legs uncrossed and stood, they were sitting down. That made me nervous and I was on edge waiting for the next time. I wasn't sure what the money baskets were for and didn't bring any money with me so I didn't know if I should be embarrassed about passing it on. The choir was singing, "Steal Away to Jesus," but I didn't see anybody take anything out of the baskets.

A man in a black robe read something with different words like *thou, didst, wouldst, thee,* and *salvation.* I didn't have a clue what he was talking about. I did understand some of his stories, but wasn't sure when he talked about Paul if it was the butcher in our market or Dan's brother. He mentioned other men like John and James. I knew several of those so I didn't know which one might have said those things. I did know about hippies who were common back then, so when the man talked about Stephen being stoned, I figured I knew what that meant.

I was so attentive and nervous I completely forgot about my little boys.

After we had done everything on the menu, I got up with everyone else and followed Alice out a side door to a patio where several hundred people were milling around drinking coffee and punch. Alice seemed to know a lot of them so she left me standing under a big tree while she socialized. I watched and listened to this interesting group of people.

I overheard some women whispering about clothes and hairdos, and it became clear that what you wore to church and what your hair looked like was very important. I decided I wouldn't come with Alice next week since I only had one dress and I feared these ladies would talk about me.

Just as I was making that decision, a man came up to me and said, "You look like you like to sing." When I said I did, he said, "Well then, you're supposed to be in the choir. I'll see you upstairs Thursday night at 7:30!" And he walked away just as quickly as he had approached me. I was shocked. I looked at the second-floor window and wondered what Dan would think if I said some man told me to meet him in the upstairs of the church on Thursday night. I didn't even know if Dan knew what a choir was (or did) since he had not been a church goer either. He said he thought his family was Serbian Orthodox but didn't know anything about it.

So that choir man wouldn't be waiting for me, I went to the church on Thursday evening to tell him I didn't think I was interested after all. But when I found the room, he told someone to pick out a robe for me before rehearsal started. Before I knew it, I was standing there in a maroon robe with a long shiny gray collar. I didn't know what to do so I did what he said and sat there with the rest of the choir, going through songs. A comforting thought went through my mind as the director talked about the Sunday service. *I wouldn't have to worry about what I wore if I was covered with a choir robe each week.* So I continued to sing in the choir.

I had so many questions about things I didn't understand. I joined a women's Bible study, thinking I'd get the answers, but the women had attended church all their lives, and some had taught Sunday school for years so they knew all the stories and could quote Scripture that didn't make any sense to me.

Since I didn't want to show my ignorance, I was quiet most of the time. Occasionally, I would ask a question, but I always felt I was interrupting the flow and throwing off their schedule. After all, they had to end at 11:00 because they were going to lunch.

~

So on the Monday following my birthday, I attended this prayer group at the United Methodist Church, like I had every Monday morning for several years. I enjoyed discussing God, the Scriptures, Jesus, prayer, and books on those subjects. However I was no longer content to exchange opinions, recipes, or the latest gossip.

Why did today seem different? Why was it irritating me to hear the same topics being hashed over and over again? What was this hollow feeling in me that seemed to be a hunger for something more? What was this itch that made me want to get up and *do* something instead of just sit there and talk about it? I couldn't understand what was wrong with me.

As women compared theologies on a certain chapter of the Bible, I wanted to scream, "Hey, we've been talking about that for months! Why don't we *do* something instead of just talk?" We'd read about the miracles Jesus performed: walking on water, raising Lazarus from the dead, healing sick people, calming the wind. We'd read that *we* could do those things – and even greater things. And then everybody turns the page and says, "Let's go to the next chapter."

Why can't I say something? Why am I just sitting here? I imagined myself shouting, "Stop! Let's put down our books for a minute and figure out how we can do these things. If we can *do* them, what are we doing just reading books *about* them?"

I opened my mouth and all that came out was, "Don't you think it would be fun to try some of these things?" How lame. Why didn't I say what I was feeling? A little later I tried again. I suggested that perhaps we could get a prayer project. All the other women looked at me like I was disrupting the class.

So I returned to my Southern California tract home with its neatly manicured lawn in a walled-in neighborhood in upper-middle-class suburbia and worked on a bazaar project and hoped the feelings would go away. I felt guilty that I didn't feel more appreciative of all the advantages in my life. I had done nothing to earn where I was. I just woke up and found myself there. *Why wasn't I happy about where I was?*

Our home for fifty years.

I grew up in an average family made up of both parents, three brothers, and a kid sister. Being born near the end of the Depression years, I recall my dad having to work long hours to make ends meet. When I think of how hard my mother also had to work to raise us five kids, I know she probably dreamed of this place where I now found myself. It would seem like heaven to her. I don't remember needing things that I didn't eventually get (wanting them, yes, but not needing them).

My family stayed to themselves, never asking for assistance or help, maybe in a way proud of their ability to manage and cope. I always felt safe and secure, even in those frightening thunderstorms and tornados that occasionally swept through Ohio. I could see how my childhood and upbringing had influenced my life. My husband, Dan, and I had built the same kind of safe haven for our children and had done so independent of any help. Ah! I was beginning to sense why it seemed so different for us than it probably did for my parents. They probably had great feelings of accomplishment and satisfaction to have been able to hold their heads high during that time when survival was not easy. They probably had worthy goals, like getting through the week. Each year brought them closer to the end of the rough times, when they might be able to save enough money for a vacation. Putting five kids through school was something to be proud of, I suppose.

Especially since my mother had a 5th grade education and my father went to school through the 8th grade. Yes, it would have been different for them.

Age 13, when I was still Marilyn.

I began to see why there was no great exhilaration about where Dan and I were. First of all, we had never had to struggle. Dan had a good job ever since we got married, and we had money in the bank. He had a good education so the fear of being out of work was not a part of our life. (Little did we know that in a few years we, too, were to experience the challenges of unemployment.)

We never even talked about goals. Oh, we might have decided that next year we would get new carpeting or trade in a car, but we had no high hopes or aspirations. "Maintain" was our middle name.

Our wedding day in 1958.

At the same time in my life, but seemingly far removed from me and my family, a town was on fire. The Watts riots broke out one week after my birthday in 1965. I remember the special news bulletins on TV saying that another fire had erupted. There were scenes of the National Guardsmen combatting rioters, people frantically running away, and firemen rushing to spray a little stream of water on a collapsing building – because of the riots there was little water pressure. All of that had nothing to do with us, or at least that is what I thought. I had never heard of Watts, even though I found out later it was only about thirty-five miles from our home. I couldn't imagine why people would behave like that, and I certainly didn't know what could be done about it.

I became bored with the TV coverage and usually used the time during news bulletins to go to the refrigerator for a snack. I had no idea that the rioting would affect me in any way.

After a few days the televisions stations began to show live coverage all day. My two daytime serials were preempted. How dare they do such a thing! I'd been watching *Young Doctor Malone* and *As the World Turns* for years. The mood of my whole day was determined by those soap operas. What right did they have use all the stations for something that didn't have anything to do with "Us"! If those people want to burn down their city, let them. (It is not without shame that I share these thoughts. I see such situations in a different light today.)

Darin and Dean, however, were more interested. To them, it was an all-day drama with sirens, guns, police cars, fire trucks, smoke, helicopters, and more. Not realizing that a diet of violence was going to affect them, I took advantage of their gravitation toward the TV each morning. I said things like, "Boys, Mommy's going to go clean the bedroom. I want you to call me if the riots are over and Mommy's programs come back on." I left them posted there to make sure I wouldn't miss anything if the riots ended.

I didn't connect some new behavior problems with their television viewing for several days. My children began to act differently. They both seemed more irritable and picky during the day, disagreeing with just about everything one could disagree with. One of them was having difficulty sleeping at night and would wake up screaming. Oh, did that infuriate me! He'd call me and call me until I went to him. I remember many a night when I'd refuse to go right away, but then I worried that my husband wouldn't get enough sleep so eventually I would have to do something.

Some nights when I felt particularly tired, I would yell, "Shut up and go to sleep!" If he continued for a while I would go back in his room and scold him saying, "There's nothing wrong with you. Now you be quiet!" (That's a pretty ridiculous thing to say to a child who's crying hysterically.) Since Dan had to get up early for work, his patience was wearing thin. Since I love to sleep, I was outraged.

One night I went into my crying son's bedroom, jerked him out of bed and went into the living room where I intended to 'have it out' with him. I sat down in the rocker with him on my lap. Because of my anger and frustration I didn't say anything. I just rocked. After a while this little boy said in a shaky little voice. "Mommy, I'm so scared. I'm so scared." That was a surprise to me. What did my kids have to be afraid of? So I asked, "What are you afraid of? What could possibly hurt you? Mommy and Daddy are here." (Which probably wasn't much comfort after the way I'd just yanked him out of bed.) "The fire, the fire, is it going to get us? Is it, Mommy? Is it, Mommy?

I began to say all the things that might appease a little boy. I told him that those fires were way far away from us (I practically pushed Watts around the globe to Vietnam) and that certainly the police and firemen could handle it. (I wanted him to think that the good guys always win in the end.) I told him that his daddy was strong and that he could ward off all the evils that might befall us. Soon my child fell asleep in my arms. I had successfully convinced him.

I gazed at his angelic face in the moonlight. There was only one problem. I hadn't convinced myself.

It was a long sleepless night for me as I wrestled with fear and uncertainty. How did I know it wasn't going to get us? What if the riots spread to our neighborhood? I had heard threats by black people in Watts (on TV) that they just might come out to suburbia and light a few fires. How did I know whether or not they were serious?

I felt upset and it seemed to be coming at the wrong time in my life. I already had problems. I was feeling mixed-up about life, and I wasn't sure what I was "supposed" to be doing. I was angry at my prayer group for not helping me or even offering to help me do something. My stomach was in a knot.

Chapter 2

How Does God Speak?

Monday morning came and I found myself at my prayer group again. The topic of the day was an upcoming retreat with our associate minister who'd promised to teach us to pray. How boring it sounded. Why would anyone want to go to "church" for forty-eight hours? I had never been on a retreat before, but it sounded to me like listening to an eight-hour sermon and then getting out our books and talking some more. *Talking*. I was sick of *talking*. Then the minister came into our meeting and told us what the retreat would be like – as nearly as he could predict a Spirit-led experience. He said he would answer any questions we had about anything that was important to us and that there would be time spent in prayer. They were actually going to do it. Not just talk about it, but *do it*!

Something stirred inside me and I knew I had to go. How would I tell Dan? Was this a good time to leave the boys? I had never left my family before. I signed up (probably the first time I ever responded to an inner prompting). I made arrangements for my family and hoped God would take care of them while I was gone. I packed my warm mountain clothes and sleeping bag and left the following morning for an experience that was to be the foundation for changing the course of my life.

The retreat was exciting from the moment we arrived at that lovely mountain cabin. There were twelve of us and everyone seemed eager to begin our discussion about prayer. I entered into it wholeheartedly because I trusted the minister to lead us into the application of what he was teaching, as he'd said he would.

Late on Saturday night, Reverend Stewart led us in a worship time during which he invited us to ask Christ into our lives (if we hadn't) or to rededicate ourselves if we'd slipped away. The mood was very sacred and I was feeling closer to God than I'd felt for a long time. There was a lot of silence that, for the first time, felt comfortable to me. It was like a dream. He invited us to pray and I remember a wave of fear sweeping over me. I'd never prayed out loud. If I was honest, I wasn't sure I'd ever prayed silently.

All of a sudden, out of the stillness, one of the women stood up and in a loud voice said, "Lord Jesus, I give my life to you. Use me in any way that is your will. Amen." She sat down. I felt a strange jealousy that she did it before I thought of it. It occurred to me that I could do it, too. My head got into an argument with my heart at the thought. *People will think you are copying.* (How crazy!) *God will think you're copying.* (Now that's *really* crazy!) *Everyone will open their eyes and look at you* (like the way I did when she stood up). *Someone will snicker* (like my classmates had in fourth grade when I said I had made up a game). Then the most frightening thought of all; God might take me seriously. Was I ready for that?

While my head and heart had this dialogue, my body (which seems to have a mind of its own) turned to stone. I felt like a statue. I couldn't move. My mouth felt welded shut. My ears were working though, because I heard the minister say "Amen" and everyone proceeded to get up and make their way to bed. I sat there wanting to yell, "Hey, rewind this film! I was just getting ready to say something or *do* something!" I felt sick. I felt left out. I'd missed my chance to do the very thing that I'd complained about them *not* doing.

Laughter and chitchat from the bunks in the bedroom annoyed me as I sat staring at the fire in the big stone fireplace. I hoped no one would notice the tears in my eyes. How could I ever go in that room with them? They were acting like kids who'd just been given free passes to Disneyland. How repulsive.

That night I looked for a quiet corner to curl up in, which I found in a room lined with bookshelves. Of all places, a library. Books. I didn't like books. In fact, there were times in my life when I hated books. I had never been a reader.

As I found a place for my sleeping bag, I flashed back to my childhood and briefly relived some of the painful times connected with reading. I had been a poor reader. Oh, I sounded good, I could pronounce all the words so the teachers often asked me to read aloud. But what no one seemed to understand was – it didn't stay in my mind. The minute I said the words they were gone. I used to feel so frustrated when I would read a whole page of history, close the book, and not even remember what country we were studying. I recall being told many times that I just wasn't trying or I was lazy. I got the impression that I wasn't very bright, and I hated myself for not being able to retain things. I used to cry in frustration and wonder why academic concepts seemed to fall out of my head.

By sixth grade, I had developed a real hatred for reading, a hatred for books, and a hatred for anyone who enjoyed reading them. I couldn't imagine anyone getting anything out of a book, so if a friend said she'd rather read than do something with me, I heard that she didn't want to be with me. I must be pretty bad company if someone would rather stare at black scratchings on a paper than be with me. Somehow I got through school with passing grades (thank goodness for extra-credit work and salt maps). In my thirty years, I don't think I had ever read a book all the way through. But there I was, choosing to be surrounded with books rather than those disgustingly happy women.

It became very quiet as the others eventually fell asleep. I lay awake for a long time. I wanted to talk to God but I wasn't sure I knew how to "get through." I'd been struggling with how to pray but was never sure of when to say "Thee" and "Thou" and that kind of thing. (This was before new versions of the Bible were popular, so most of us had the King James Version.) I had never said a prayer out loud before because I was afraid of making a mistake. If only I could get the prayer I felt in my heart up and out of my mouth, or at least clear my mind.

Slowly the words began to form and I whispered my first real prayer. *"Oh Lord, I don't know what I'm supposed to be doing with my life. I'm beginning to suspect that you had a reason for creating me at this time in history and in my particular situation. But what is it Lord? If there's something you want me to be doing, how will I know what that something is? How do you speak to people, Lord?"*

My mind flashed to my prayer group and how some of the women would arrive some mornings and say, "The Lord spoke to me last night," or "I talked it over with Jesus and he said…" I would become irritated and sort of tune out whatever they said, while saying in my mind, "I bet they're just saying that. Why would God speak to her? I felt like saying, "Oh, he did not!" I was jealous of their relationship with him. I couldn't stand to think that he talked to them and he didn't talk to me. If he really did talk to them, did that mean he loved them more than me? I shook my head in order to quit thinking about it and went back to my faltering prayer. *"Father, how do you talk to your children? How do you communicate, Lord? How would I know if you wanted something of me?"*

I don't remember if I was talking aloud or in my mind but I know that I poured out many questions that night without knowing if anyone was really listening. The moonlight caused the room almost to glow and I looked at the thousands of books lining the walls. Titles and authors meant nothing to me, they simply created a colorful design that my eyes enjoyed scanning for a few moments. At some point, my eyes stopped. I wondered why that little blue book looked out of place where it was. All the other books were arranged in graduated sizes, except for one that was wedged between two big volumes of something. Thinking back, I wonder why I even noticed it – there must have been hundreds of blue books. I felt drawn to get up and go over and look at it, and for once I didn't talk myself out of it. (That may have been the first miracle in my life.) I quietly crawled out of my sleeping bag, went directly to the little book, pulled it off the shelf and let it fall open somewhere in the middle. The words on the page were distinct in the moonlight. As I read, I felt a gentle surge of electricity flow through my body. The words bore deep into my soul.

My child, you have been going from person to person seeking Me. Now seek the Light instead of the lamp! I am the Way, the Truth, and the Life.

My heart almost stopped. Those words went to my very core. I closed the little blue book, looked up, and said aloud, "Oh God, you're here!" Again, I opened the book.

I want my children to hear My words above all others. You find it hard to believe that I can speak directly to you today. I speak to many who do not hear - who do not want to hear. I tell you, by greatly desiring, by singleness of purpose, by purity of heart, you can hear My words.

God was talking to me. Many questions started spinning in my mind. *How was this happening? Who put this book here? Was it just for me? What if I hadn't chosen this room? Should I open the book a third time?* Certainly all the pages wouldn't apply to me. It was probably a coincidence. I slowly opened it again.

I call you to a life of joy, the joy that the mountains at sunset, the birds in the lofty pines, know and express.

That did it. Why would it mention mountains and pine trees? My eyes turned toward the window with the moonbeams shining in. I could see the towering pines just outside, and yes, I heard a bird.

Joy flooded through me as I returned to my bed. My mind was clear. I felt loved in a new way. I wanted to *sing.* Instead, I said very quietly, "Lord, you are here, aren't you! You do hear me when I call, don't you! I love you, Lord. I want to do your will. *Do* it, Lord, not just talk about it. Please guide me in the coming days. Oh Jesus, will you walk with me? And teach me? I give you my life, Lord, and tomorrow, I'm reporting for duty!" I went to sleep feeling like a child with a secret.

Chapter 3

The Call

I was awakened by the morning sun warming me. The songs of birds reminded me of my promise and of God's promise to speak to me. I could hardly wait to get up and begin my new adventure, but something told me to linger a while and pray that I would be receptive.

I felt prompted to open the book again. It had lain on my pillow all night. This time it said,

To my children I speak in many ways; through My words recorded in the Bible; through the words of My saints of every land, of every century; through sudden convictions in the hearts of those who follow Me. Listen...listen. This is the dawn of a new day. Listen for My will. Desire only My will.

"Oh Father," I prayed, "I will try to hear you today in all of the events, in all of my dealings, in what I read and hear others say, in the wind and clouds and trees. O God, help me to listen with new ears. And help me to heed what I hear."

The smell of coffee and the lighthearted chatter in the kitchen eventually lured me out of bed to join the other women. I was startled at how beautiful they looked. My heart felt warm when I realized how very much they each meant to me. The embraces seemed genuine and there was much eagerness to begin the new day.

The retreat ended at noon with a communion service. During it, I reminded God that I had given my life to him and that as soon as I got home I would be looking for clues as to what he wanted me to do. For the first time I felt as though I understood communion. I accepted by faith that I was forgiven and that through the body and blood of our Lord Jesus Christ I was a new creature. I believed it. Now I had to *be* it and *live* it.

The drive down the mountain with five women talking at the same time found me silently reliving my experience the night before. I wanted to savor it. I wondered if I should tell the others about it. Instead I just monitored the questions that began to bubble up in my mind. Will God really speak to me? Will I recognize his voice?

His voice! Why had I always imagined he would sound like a *man*? Will he speak English? I realized I had really limited God up until now. I recalled one time when I raced home from prayer group after one of the members told about God speaking to her. I ran into my bedroom and said, "OK, God. If you spoke to her, why don't you speak to me?" I waited and waited and nothing happened. I guess the only thing I would have settled for was a man's voice. In English.

The next thing I knew, the car was pulling into my driveway and my boys and husband were coming out to greet me. "Did you have a good time?" "Was there any snow?" "Did you miss us?" "Hurry and get ready!"

Get ready? For what? Oh, no! How could I have forgotten? If I have to go to that potluck supper I'm going to lose this wonderful spiritual feeling.

Then I remembered. We were in charge of it. Grudgingly, I threw together a casserole while Dan helped the boys get ready. Under my breath I told God that he'd have to wait until this was over before I could listen to him. I was certain he didn't attend potluck suppers.

Five minutes before we went out the door, the phone rang and I was informed that our guest speaker wouldn't be able attend that evening. *Now what?* I wondered. *I hope they don't expect me to entertain them.* In the mood I was in, I'd probably tell them to go back home because they were ruining my retreat experience.

When we arrived at the church we found out that a replacement speaker, a Reverend Mr. Cooper, was on his way. No one knew anything about him, who he was or where he was from, let alone what he would talk about.

It turned out that young Reverend Cooper was from a church in the heart of Los Angeles. A ghetto. A slum. A neighborhood so crowded there was hardly room to breathe. He told about his parish; the ten thousand people living in the shadow of the tall, impressive downtown office buildings. His church had no congregation – everyone had moved away. He proceeded to take us on a trip to the ghetto, via his slide projector.

I found myself interested enough to keep my eyes open. The room was dark and everyone's attention was fixed on the large screen on the stage. We saw where people lived: shacks, dilapidated hotels, old rundown houses, broken-down cars, alleyways. *How can people live like that? Why doesn't somebody do something about it?*

Faces. Faces always get to me. Reverend Cooper began to introduce us to some of his friends in the inner city. There was Marcy, the daughter of a prostitute, and Barbara, the mother of eight children, Arnold, the alcoholic, who slept in the alley, and Marcus, who wanted to learn to read. On and on went the parade of faces with problems beyond what my mind could comprehend. Yet, I was engrossed in their stories.

Mr. Cooper told about each person in such a way that I felt I knew them. He really loved them. I wondered if he *had* to work there or if he chose to.

Maybe it was the story of the old woman whose two sons had been shot in the riots that brought tears to my eyes, I don't know. It could have been seeing the little children loitering on the church steps looking so forlorn. Something was causing a deep sadness to well up inside me. The speaker's voice faded in and out as I searched for a Kleenex, pretending I was blowing my nose.

Suddenly, I became aware of a thumping in my chest. I began to feel warm. Uncomfortable. A thought pierced my mind. What if God asked me to go to a place like that? The thought made my heart beat even faster. I was gripping the chair. My knuckles felt numb.

I looked around the darkened room and got the impression that everyone was waiting for a commercial. At least they were

19

looking at the screen and not me. The thought returned. What if God called me to service in that place? Would I go? Could I go? I began to argue with God in my mind. "Lord, you'd never expect me to go to the ghetto, would you? You know my little kids need me at home. And you know, Lord, how Dan doesn't like for me to be gone very much. Lord, you wouldn't expect me to do something I don't know how to do, would you? And so far from home. Lord, I've never even driven on the freeway by myself! You wouldn't, would you, Lord? Lord?"

In that moment a strange feeling swept over me. I realized that maybe he would. I fell limp in my seat. Now what was I going to do? Was this really God? I thought he didn't attend potlucks. Why did I come here anyway?

During the rest of the presentation I built a good case in my mind against going by reminding God that I had no education to train me for such work. I wasn't a teacher, nurse, psychologist, social worker, or the like. What could an ordinary housewife from Garden Grove do? I'm a *nobody*! I can't do anything!

The blinding lights brought me back to reality. I wanted to get up and run, but Mr. Cooper had a few closing remarks. "I suppose some of you are wondering what you might do to help. You're probably saying to yourself, 'I'm not a professional, I have no credentials, so what can I do?' Well, let me tell you what I really need." I couldn't believe it. He was reading my mind. No fair! "What I really need," he continued, "is someone who is willing to come to my neighborhood and listen to people. They need to be listened to. They need to know someone cares. I'm praying that God will send someone to us."

He had just destroyed my argument. I wanted to get out of there. Maybe I need sleep. I've been up a long time.

As I stood up to retrieve my casserole dish, for a moment I had the fear that it was somehow rigged, that Mr. Cooper would see me and say, "There she is. She's the one."

"Pardon me. Excuse me." I worked my way through the crowd and escaped to the car.

An hour later I was curled up in bed with a pillow over my head, not knowing what kind of night I had in store for me. I tossed and turned. Could it possibly have been God? Here I was, twenty-four hours after I'd given my life to him and asked him to guide me, and now I didn't want to believe that he'd actually do it. I remembered how critical I'd been of my prayer group members for not doing anything. Wow, I'm glad I didn't tell them about my promise to God. I'd never live it down. I prayed myself to sleep. "Dear God, you know me and my situation here. Do you really want me to leave this and go to help those people? O God, I'm scared! Is it OK to be scared, Lord? I feel so inadequate, so out of it. You know, Lord, how much I love my kids and how much they seem to need me."

At that point I just lay there and watched scenes in my mind. It was as though God said to me, "Fear not, my child, for I am with you and will go before you. It is *because* you love your children that I call you to care about the world they will grow up in." Of course… I must be thinking about the world my sons will inherit. Why had I not thought of that before? My awareness had never gone beyond our four walls until this week, and now God wants me to s-t-r-e-t-c-h.

"OK, Lord, I'll try. I want to trust you with my life. Thank you for speaking to me. I will try to be obedient." I slept.

Chapter 4

Into the Ghetto

The next day was Monday, the beginning of a new week and also the day my prayer group met. Before the group began I asked if I could share something. A hush fell over them as I told first about my encounter with God on the retreat and then about my feeling of being led to work in the ghetto. They listened and *heard*.

Several of them encouraged me to go, even if it was just for a visit. Why hadn't I thought of that? A visit.

"Hey, why don't we all go? It could be like a field trip. We could take canned goods and clothes to donate to the church where Mr. Cooper works." Everyone seemed enthusiastic. (I *knew* sooner or later I'd get them to do a project!)

Within a few days things were arranged and six of us women, with assorted children, drove north on the Santa Ana Freeway to a place we'd never been. Because I had a large station wagon (before seatbelts), I drove. I wasn't sure whether or not to tell them I'd never driven on the freeway before (my husband was always willing to do it). As it ended up, they wouldn't have heard me anyway – with the kids laughing and wiggling and the women all talking at once.

As we reached the halfway point between Garden Grove and Los Angeles, my anxiety level began to rise. I became aware of a strange phenomenon taking place inside me. It was as though I was divided into three parts and they were all arguing, all talking at the same time. I tried to sort out what I was feeling and somehow inwardly hearing.

My *heart* seemed to be saying, yes, yes, this is right. Trust it. Every feeling inside me seemed to be chanting, go, go, go! I imagined that God was saying, "Finally, you are listening to me." I felt adventuresome, courageous. So courageous that I pushed down on the accelerator and noticed that my leg was shaking. Somebody said "What's wrong with the car? It's kind of thumping." I tuned into my body and began to get a very different message than the one I'd just gotten from my heart. My legs were trembling, my knees shaking. My foot was uncontrollable on the gas pedal. I was perspiring and my head was throbbing. My clammy hands felt slippery on the steering wheel.

I knew that if my *body* could have talked in that moment it would have shouted, "Go back home where it's safe! Go someplace and hide. Relax. Be comfortable!" Which part should I listen to? My feelings or my body? There seemed to be such a contradiction in me.

While I was trying to decide, a third voice rose from within me to be heard. My *mind* had a message all its own. The second I tuned into it I heard, "Boy, is this stupid! You're going to get yourself killed! Oh, are you ever dumb to think you could do anything to help! What will the neighbors think? What will Dan think?"

Dan. I saw a mental picture of him coming home from work and finding the note I left. "Honey, I've gone to the ghetto to see what I can do." *Oh, dear. Why did I leave a note like that? He'll probably faint. I am so dumb. I am stupid. O God, help me get home before he does. Help! There's a war going on inside of me. A riot has broken out! Help!*

I felt so fragmented it was all I could do just to keep driving, hoping someone would tell me when to turn off because I certainly had no clue. "There's a familiar street," someone in the back seat said. We'd heard Mr. Cooper mention it. I was so eager to get off the freeway that I cut across two lanes of traffic without even looking, and I decided to trust the Lord that our destination was nearby. (Thank you, Lord, for that demonstration of your divine protection.)

What a different world. I found it hard to believe. I had never thought of people living under the freeway off-ramps and overpasses. How many times Dan and I had gone to Los Angeles to the museum or farmers' market on the same freeway. To think there are people living in a slum down under and out of view.

I drove slowly so we could look at the surroundings. Would we find the old church building we'd seen in the slides? I felt strange, looking at people – as if I was invading their privacy. But they got even with us, because they stared at us too.

Someone suggested we park and walk around. Had they gone mad? Get out? Here? What if someone asks us who we are? Or why we're here? What would we say? (Oh dear God, what *are* we doing here?)

We parked. *Now what? Everybody's looking at us. Should we get out? Am I the only one who is afraid?* The children were singing, "This old man, he played one..." The women were commenting on the style of an apartment building. The next thing I knew, someone was telling the kids we were going for a walk. I was to discover another part of myself in a few moments.

But first, a brainstorm. I had a great idea. "Listen, everybody. When we get out I think we should act like we know where we're going so the neighborhood people won't think we're just snooping around. Here's my plan. Let's walk down to that corner very confidently, as if we have business here. When we get to the light we turn the corner so the people along here can't see us. We walk with heads held high along that street to the next corner and turn, so those people think we know what we're doing. We do it for two more blocks until we get back to our car. How's that?" I was pleased how well I controlled my voice. I sounded cool as a cucumber. I got up on my knees in the front seat so I could be heard way in the back of the station wagon. "Kids," I said, "we're going to get out here and go for a little walk."

They all started yelling things like "I don't want to" and "Why?" and "I have to go to the bathroom" and "When are we going to eat?"

All of a sudden I lost it and screamed, "You kids shut up! You get out there and stand in line. Don't you talk or ask any more questions." My face felt hot. "Now don't you run ahead and don't you lag behind and don't you talk to strangers. Just shut up and do as I tell you!" *Where did that come from? Did that really come out of me?* Judging from the shocked looks on their faces (the kids and the mothers), it must have. I felt humiliated.

Nevertheless, it worked. The children got out of the car. They stood in a straight line and there wasn't a sound. While the women debated whether they should take their sweaters and the kids decided to get apples out of their lunch sacks, I said a quick prayer. "Now God, I've come this far and it hasn't been easy. We're going to take this walk, so you have exactly four blocks to tell me what I'm doing here. If we get back to this car and I haven't heard from you, I'm going to go home and never come back. You hear that, God?" I still couldn't believe he was aware of all this.

After the hassle of getting everyone out of the car, throwing stuff back in, somebody forgetting something, and so on, we finally slammed the doors and started walking. We did great for the first fifteen steps and then one of the mothers said, "By the way, I locked all the doors so no one would steal anything."

When I hear the word *lock* I froze in my tracks. A wave of fear swept through me as I turned and announced that I had left the keys on the floor of the car. Our mission of mercy was immediately abandoned. We raced back to the car and proceeded to try to break in with nail files and bobby pins.

I felt like Job in the Bible when he said, "And the thing I feared came upon me." A crowd gathered. Every two minutes someone was asking the two questions I couldn't answer: "Who are you?" "What are you doing here?" I wanted to scream, "How would I know!" Instead I concentrated on my amateur lock-picking skills until the police came. Honestly, officer, it's *our* car. For a person who didn't want to be stared at, breaking into a car was not the way to avoid attention.

My body temperature was rising as the police called the neighborhood fire department to help them break in to get the keys and check the registration. As the crowd grew in size, I found myself hiding in the shadows under the archway of a building. Where was God?

Soon the fireman opened the door, then all four doors. The crowd applauded. We said, "Oh, we don't want to get in, officer." Most of the crowd shrugged their shoulders, shook their heads and walked away. But the neighborhood children hung around for a while. Our kids started saying "Hi" to them and they answered back. A few women stood nearby as though they were keeping an eye on their children until these strangers moved on.

I could understand their concern so I walked over to them and said in a calm voice, "We don't know why we're here. We aren't anyone special, but we live in a different town and we wanted to visit your neighborhood and get acquainted with some of you." Completely honest. Why hadn't I thought of that sooner? I went on to say that we hoped to learn about their community and that with their permission we'd like to visit them every week to get to know them better.

I couldn't believe what I was hearing myself say. I had thought we were there to try to "help" these people and there I was saying we'd come to learn from *them*. I don't know how that came out of my mouth because I'd never thought of it before. It made me think that perhaps God was involved with this after all.   I imagined they would be excited that these neat-looking mothers with pretty children had come all this way to get acquainted with them. Shock. They just stared at us.

"Can you tell us about your neighborhood? Or can we walk around and look at it?" we asked.

"Yeah, go ahead."

So we wandered around for a while with the neighbor-hood children trailing behind (to our children's delight). Eventually we found the old church we'd seen in the slides.

I experienced my second shock when the minister didn't seem overly enthralled with our presence either. We found him up to his neck in rummage in the church basement. Signs out in front announced a Giant Rummage Sale. After we got his attention, we said, "Hello! Here we are! We came to help the people in the ghetto!"

His blank stare made me realize he'd probably shown his slides to hundreds of groups, so why did I expect him to say, "Oh, you're the folks from Garden Grove!"

What could we do? Somehow his telling us we could sort rummage didn't set right. "We mean out in the community. We want to help with those kinds of things."

Whoever would have thought we'd be spending the day going door to door in 100-degree heat, inviting people to a rummage sale? I felt hollow as I fearfully knocked on each door. This neighborhood was made up of many different ethnic groups: Mexican, Oriental, Black, Italian, German, and more. Some people were suspicious. Some were friendly. Some just closed the door. Some said, "Thank you."

Inside, I felt let down. I thought Reverend Cooper would welcome us with open arms, maybe even cry. I wanted him to fall down on his knees and say, "Thank you, God, for sending these friends here." Oh, well. This door-knocking thing wasn't what I had in mind as a new career either. In the weeks to come, I was to learn many things about myself.

Chapter 5

My Eyes are Opened

A new era in my life began. That trip was the first of many we were to make to that inner-city community and the Reverend Mr. Cooper's church. It was never again as difficult as it was the first time.

Sometimes I would drive to the old church and sit on the front steps with my guitar and sing with the neighborhood children. We didn't see much of Mr. Cooper, since he spent most of his time out in the parish as a sort of troubleshooter.

Yet we began to make friends we could talk to. With a sense of wide-eyed wonder, I visited the women we met on that first day. I spent time in their apartments, watching their children play. I listened to despair and frustration as it seeped out through the small talk. They became my teachers, and I learned many things.

I met mothers who knew nothing about childcare or about family planning, since this was before the days of free birth-control advice. I held babies who had diaper rash from their toes to their noses because their mothers didn't know what to do about it. I watched two-year-olds being given a bottle of curdled milk since the family didn't have a refrigerator. The bigger kids got whatever food there was. I was excited at the thought that perhaps I could help with some of these problems. I had a background of Dr. Spock, *Parents' Magazine*, TV, and a mother who seemed to know all sorts of inexpensive home remedies.

Many women in that neighborhood couldn't even tell time. None had watches and few had clocks in their apartments. I was puzzled why women never showed up on time for meetings or gatherings. When I felt comfortable enough with Barbara to ask why she wasn't more interested in knowing the time of day or the date, she replied, "Every day is the same. Nothing happens. I have no place to go, no one comes to visit, I have nothing to do. Besides, what difference does anything make?"

"Barbara," I said, "you must have something in your life that you don't want to miss. Isn't there something you look forward to?"

Her answer haunted me for days, "Yeah, I look forward to dying."

How could it be? Someone the same age as I. All of a sudden I had all these things to live for. How could a life be so empty? "O Lord, help me to help Barbara find a reason to go on living. A reason, Lord. Something exciting."

In the days to come I found many things to do. I learned that the women were consistently being shortchanged by the traveling bread vendors who honked their horns every morning looking for customers. If I went out to the curb and stood there with the customer, the man's ability to do math seemed to improve.

It's strange how before I went to the inner city I used to think, "But what can I do? I don't know anything about their problems. There's no way *I* could help!" How different it is after you arrive. The question of "What can I do?" never comes up. If you see a mother of five kids pushing a grocery cart six blocks home from the store, you simply help her or pick up one of the kids. If you see a blind man afraid to cross the busy street, you take his arm and lead him across. If a child is lost, you take her door to door until you find out where she belongs. If someone is sick and he has no phone to call a doctor, you find out where one is and take him there. It seemed so simple once I was actually doing it. And no one asked to see my credentials.

It became apparent that many of the people could not read. God answered my prayers for someone to come and teach them to read and write. I was introduced to a woman named Helen Line who told me she taught Laubach Literacy teacher training. She told about the groups of people she'd trained to establish literacy centers where adults could learn in an atmosphere of love and encouragement. And within a few weeks a literacy class was started for would-be teachers to learn how to be tutors, since the Laubach method advocates for a close, caring relationship between teacher and student.

The apartment building near Watts, LA, where we rented a room so we could spend more time with the folks we were getting to know.

After a few weeks we opened our Literacy Center in Rev. Cooper's church. I'll never forget my first student. I showed up at the church that day with my workbooks and a bag of objects that were part of the first reading lesson. I set up a table with tablet and pencil neatly arranged next to the student's workbook. The other teachers were at their tables awaiting their first students. I wondered who I'd get.

One by one people began to arrive in response to the flyers that were passed out by neighborhood children. One of my friends was acting as hostess and introducing the new person to one of the teachers. I watched as each of my friends were coupled with a student. I was the only teacher without one.

Finally, a woman came through the door – a short, plump, troubled-looking lady in her fifties, whose drab housedress seemed to match the color of her skin. "Lord, she's not the one I want! I want someone young! Lord, they're telling me she doesn't speak any English, only Spanish. Help! I don't know one single word of Spanish! Lord, here she comes. They're bringing her to me. Where are you, Lord?" I wanted to run.

Mrs. Aguilar was introduced to me, and neither of us smiled as she sat down across from me. We stared at each other, not knowing what to do. My eyes pretended to be busy. I gazed at the workbook and my little objects neatly placed there. How could I start? I had rehearsed how I would begin so many times in the last week, anticipating this moment.

I glanced around the room and saw my friends with their students, some of whom were also Mexican. I saw a Spanish-English dictionary on a table nearby and stepped over to pick it up. I was sure that Mrs. Aguilar could hear my heart pounding from the fear that filled me. A thought flashed through my mind: "Tell her you're afraid." Why would I do a thing like that? Again it came: "Tell her you're afraid." While I was thumbing through the dictionary, my head was saying "How will she ever respect me as her teacher if she knows I'm scared?"

I found the word for "teacher," and kept my finger between the pages as I searched for "afraid." OK, Lord, here goes.

My voice quivered as I somehow pronounced those two words. I felt too dumb to look directly at her for what seemed like an eternity. I looked at her hands, twisting each other. My eyes traveled up her dark-skinned arms to her slumped shoulders and then her face. There were tears in her eyes. Her face began to soften. She opened her mouth and, like a waterfall, words came tumbling out. Spanish words.

One of my friends who could speak a little Spanish came over and said, "She's telling you, 'Thank you, thank you,' for saying you're afraid because she is very frightened also. She wants to learn to speak English so much, but she's afraid she's too old. She says she started toward the church three times, but didn't have the courage to open the door. The fourth time, she made herself come in. She prayed that God would give her a good teacher and she is now saying, 'Thank you, God.' "

When I heard that, *I* wanted to cry. We ended up hugging each other while our tears turned to laughter. We sat back down, took a deep breath, and she wrote her name on her workbook. The lesson was underway.

~

Months went by, yet my friends and I diligently kept returning to the place that had captured our hearts, to the people who were breaking our hearts. We were gaining more and more insight into the problems our inner-city friends face. We knew we couldn't look for solutions until we understood what the problems were.

I became friends with a young mother who taught me something valuable. Lupe was a challenge at first, not because of her learning disability, but because of my not wanting to work very close to her. You see, Lupe had worn the same clothes for four months and her body odor seemed unbearable. I didn't want to offend her or lose her as a student. When truckloads of clothing were delivered to the inner-city church for a rummage sale, compliments of several middle-class suburban churches, I got the idea of taking Lupe as my guest and treating her to some pretty new clothes. The big rummage sale was planned for the same day that Lupe and I usually met for our lesson. It seemed natural to say, "Hey, Lupe, let's go see what they have at the rummage sale." No response. "Don't you think that's a good idea?"

"I'll go if *you* want to go," she said, "but *I* don't need anything.

I was baffled by her lack of interest. I was sure she'd get excited after she saw the neat things I'd noticed on the days I'd helped to sort and price things. But I gave up after asking her six times if she liked something and would like me to buy it for her. Her answers were always, "Yes" and "No." Yes, she liked it, and No, she didn't want it.

As we walked back to her apartment, where she spent most of her time with her two babies, I shared my disappointment with her. I said I had so hoped to buy her something as a gift. In the cool of the evening she began to share with me something that was to open my eyes to a new level of understanding.

"I don't need anything. These clothes are all I got, but they're enough. I don't have a washer, or a dryer, or an iron. I don't even have a place to hang clothes." Her voice trailed off. There were tears in her eyes. "And besides, why dress up when nobody cares?"

I felt as if I'd been stabbed. I ached to say, "Oh, Lupe, I do! I care!" But the words just wouldn't come out of my mouth. In the coming weeks, however, I became determined to show her how much I cared, and I saw a miracle one day as I sat in the church basement waiting for her. In the door came a lovely woman in a flowered blouse and neat slacks. I would have sworn it was Lupe. My mind argued and said it couldn't be. Lupe's hair always looked like an explosion and this person's hair was neatly pulled back and held by a red rubber band. She came over to my table and stood looking at me. My heart skipped a beat.

"Lupe!" I said, trying to control the shock in my voice. "You look beautiful! What's happened to you?" She drew me to my feet by extending her hand and threw her arms around me. "I wanted to dress up for my teacher because I'm so happy! Now somebody cares!" Oh God, how could I have been a part of such transformation? I actually saw her change from a caterpillar into a butterfly right before my eyes. Thank you, Lord, for what you are teaching me through these beautiful people – these hurting, frustrated, lonely, beautiful people.

Chapter 6

Public Speaking

After two-and-a-half years of involvement in the inner-city church and other places this led to, I began to get weary. The fact that everything looked the same and the problems still remained made me wonder if I was accomplishing anything. Was I doing this work just to salve my conscious? It didn't seem that I was making a difference.

My home life was beginning to show signs of gross neglect. My family didn't want to hear my stories anymore. I began to feel martyred and alone. Lord, what is this feeling? Are you calling me to leave the city? Or am I giving up? I really don't know Lord, I had thought you led me to this place.

In time, I was to learn that when God leads me to something or someone, it's not necessarily to stay there all my life, but to go through it and learn the lessons it has for me. Sometimes I have trouble remembering to ask God if and when he wants me to quit something and move on. Ruts can give a sense of security.

During this time of questioning, I received an invitation to speak to a PTA group at a nearby school. At first that seemed more frightening than working in the ghetto. Then I realized that when I was working with people in the ghetto, there was a great need. I often knew things they didn't know simply because of my upbringing. But it was a different story in my own community. I'd always felt inadequate because I hadn't gone on to college. I felt dumb and inferior around educated people. I'd never thought of myself as attractive and I didn't wear clothes with impressive labels. My nervousness was caused by the fear that the other women would talk about me or not like me. Or that I'd say something using poor grammar and people would laugh (or worse, look disgusted). Lord, are you in this?

I mulled the offer over for a few days, and in that time I was reminded of my prayer of commitment to God, that I'd go anywhere he wanted me to go.

So, in a few weeks I made my debut as a public speaker. I took slides of some of my inner-city friends, their houses, the abandoned church, etc., and was going to give a simple talk about how the situation looked through the eyes of an untrained, unskilled, unknowledgeable, scared housewife. In preparation I had written out three pages of narration. I didn't realize I couldn't read them with the lights out. Fortunately, I had put the slides in an order that would remind me what to say.

Afterward, people came up to me and told me how moved they were by my presentation. Two people invited me to speak to their organizations: one a church, the other a Rotary Club.

As the weeks went by, it seemed that this was what God wanted me to do. For over two years God had evidently wanted me to comfort the afflicted, and now, he was calling me to afflict the comfortable.

I was desperately trying to help people understand the plight of those in the ghetto. It was 1968 and there was so much racial tension following the riots in LA, and people were divided about what should be done. Somehow I had to find a way to get to the hearts of the listeners in my affluent audiences. So I sat down at my old Royal typewriter and typed up a script for an encounter I had with a young boy in front of Temple Church in LA. I played the part of both characters, walking back and forth across the stage when appropriate. (This would became my signature presentation for ten years, shared in churches, schools, camps, and social clubs of all kinds, sometimes three or four times a week. I'm sure I told it more than 500 times. And every time I cried.)

What is God Like?

This is a conversation between two very different people: a woman from a suburban community (me), and a dirty, straggly, Mexican-Negro boy from the slums of the inner city. Miguel spends a lot of time sitting on a box next to an apartment building where he can watch the people and cars go by. Every Saturday he watches for a lady to park her car and enter an old empty church building on the corner. He always wants to talk to her, but usually only gets up enough courage to say, "Hi, Lady." She looks friendly, but she was always in a hurry. But one day he gets brave enough.

Hey, Lady, what is God like?

Well, Miguel, He's like a father.

Gee, Lady, my old man's a drunk and he beats us all the time! When he's home, that is. Most of the time he goes away for days and days. Is God like that?

(Looking embarrassed) Oh, NO Miguel... Ah, you must have a mother?

I got a mother, alright, but when she's not out lookin' for work, she's with her boyfriends. She's always hollerin' at my sister and me. I don't think she likes us! She's always sayin', "If it weren't for you damn kids, I wouldn't have to walk all day lookin' for a job!" How come she blames us? We didn't ask to be born! We don't eat much... just what's left on the plates in the morning when she and her boyfriends leave. Why doesn't she like us, Lady?

(Becoming nervous) Oh, honey, she likes you, I'm sure. She's just trying to support you and your sister. It isn't easy nowadays. I have trouble myself making ends meet, with prices as high as they are. Oh, I'm sure she likes you.

Well, what's He like, Lady? You're carrying a Bible, so you must know! My mom used to have a Bible, but she threw it in the trash ... she said it wasn't meant for people like us... we can't read or write so good ... or do nothin' for nobody else.

Think of someone who loves you Miguel, did you ever feel loved by anyone? (a long silence) Maybe an aunt? Or an uncle? Or a teacher ... or a neighbor? Anybody?

I had this dog once, Lady. I know *he* loved me. You shoulda' seen the way he looked at me when I held him real close. I *know* he loved me. I found him on the street one day ... he was so cold and skinny. I used to just sit here and hold him ... 'til he died. I wish someone would hold *me* like I held that dog!

(With surprise) Miguel, didn't anyone ever hold you?

(Shyly) Naw ... (with surprise) Wait a minute! Someone had to when I was a baby didn't they? Yeh, I know they did ... cause my mom said she gave me away once when I was real little but the people gave me back cause they couldn't afford me either. But they had to hold me then, didn't they? But I don't remember. Lady, you still haven't told me. What's He like? You know ... don't you?

(Becoming more exasperated) Of course I know! But ... but ... it's hard to explain. (Pacing back and forth, she snaps her fingers as an idea comes.) Miguel! Did you ever look up at the beautiful sky? Did you ever see the birds fly? Did you ever go for a walk in the woods and see a beautiful mountain stream?

Yeh, I look up lots of times ... and if it ain't too smoggy, sometimes I see a jet plane! Hey, where do they go? I ain't ever been out of my neighborhood, but someday I'm gonna' go far, far away on a jet ... ain't never comin' back. Yeh, I look up! I see all these old apartment buildings with dirty, broken windows ... with people lookin' out ... old people ... sick people ... little people, too little to get out. You ask about a woods? I ain't never been in a woods before. Is a stream anything like the gutter? If it ain't, I guess I don't know what you're talkin' about. How come you're askin' all these questions? Why won't you tell me about God?

(Getting irritated) Well, Miguel, if you'll just give me time! It's not easy to explain ... you just don't understand ... I'm trying to tell you, but ... I'll just have to think about it for a minute ... (Becoming increasingly more tense and nervous) I go to church every Sunday and teach Sunday School. Those children understand me – why don't you?

I used to think I knew what God was like ... all by myself! My sister and me used to sit on the steps of that old church when there was people in it. We never went in ... I guess we didn't dress right or somethin' ... maybe we was the wrong color. The people used to step right over us or walk past us like they didn't even see us. Like we didn't have a face. We could hear the man talkin' and the people singin'... and ya know? I almost started believin' some of that junk! But boy, I know better now!

What do you mean "junk?" What do you mean, you know better now?

You know, Lady ... like 'God will take care of you.' (angrily) Boy, that's a lie! How about 'Take it to the Lord in prayer" ... What's He gonna' do about it? He ain't done nothin' for us! The only song they sang that made a little sense was "Onward Christian Soldiers" cause everybody marched out of that church and went someplace! Now it's empty. HEY, LADY, DID THEY TAKE

GOD WITH 'EM WHEN THEY WENT? DOES GOD LIVE WHERE YOU LIVE?

(Looking worried and frightened) Oh, Miguel, I thought He did … I thought He did! But you really make me wonder! (She wanders away a little ways and looks up with her hands clasped and gasps…) Oh, God, help me … help me …what shall I say? (After a moment of silence, she seems to get a great idea … a calm sweeps over her and with much enthusiasm, she returns to the boy.) Miguel, you want to know about God … well, do you want to know where He is right now? Right this very minute? (very excited) Well, He's RIGHT HERE! Honestly, Miguel … He's right here … He … He just told me! REALLY!! You've got to believe me … He loves you and he loves me … and He's right here! WHAT DO YOU THINK OF THAT MIGUEL? (Excitement leaves her face when she notices the boy does not respond. A look of panic comes across her face.) You do believe me, don't you? You do believe me, don't you, Miguel?

I … I … don't know. I just don't know. I want to believe you, HONEST!

(With a look of love) Oh Son, come here … please … I want to hold you. Will you let me? Oh, really, I WANT to. Please come here and let me hold you. (He backs away as she reaches out, she looks hurt. Then with excitement…) Miguel, maybe we could find God together! Because I think I lost Him too! Please come here (with arms outstretched) and let me hold you. Maybe we can find Him together … please?

(Hesitating) Ah … ah … should we go into the church?

NO, Son, God's not just in a church! In fact … maybe God can't get into some churches. Oh, maybe I shouldn't say that, but … really, I wonder. I'll bet God tries, but people don't let him! Or they let Him in and then don't want to let Him out. But I KNOW

He tries ... He LOVES us! (almost begging) Please come here, Son ... I want to hold you.

(Longing to go, but still hesitating) I want to believe ... honest ... I want to. But how can I know for sure?

(As though another idea comes to her) I just realized something! Do you know how I found out what God was like? When I was little like you ... from people who loved me very much. They showed me what He was like. HEY, THAT'S IT! PEOPLE HAVE TO BE SHOWN ... NOT TOLD! THEY MUST FEEL GOD AND NOT JUST LISTEN ABOUT HIM!
(She boldly walks over and takes him in her arms. They embrace and relax in each other's arms. She becomes overjoyed ... sort of laughing through her tears.) How do you feel, Son? Do you feel kind of good inside? Do you feel warm ... and safe ... at least for this minute? THAT'S GOD, MIGUEL! Do you feel sort of like laughing and crying at the same time? THAT"S GOD, Miguel! I think He sent me to you. Honestly, I think God sent me to you to answer your prayers. Isn't that great? He's using me to answer your prayers!
(A worried look comes upon her face and she holds him back and looks into his face.) Oh, Son, I'm sorry I didn't come any sooner. I'm sorry you had to wait a long time. Oh yes, I'm sorry ...but I was so busy ... or ... I thought I was ... that I didn't hear Him call me. (Again she holds him close.) BUT MIGUEL, I'M HERE NOW! YES, I'M HERE NOW! ISN'T IT GREAT ... I'M HERE NOW. (She wipes his tears.) Thank God, I'm here now. AMEN

~

More and more doors opened for speaking opportunities. I didn't know statistics or percentages of budgets or government programs and the like. All I knew was what I had experienced, and what I had felt. Each time I prayed about whether I was to accept another speaking engagement, the answer seemed to be yes, even though my speaking to so many groups meant that I no longer had time to visit my friends in the inner city as often.

41

And I didn't have as much time for my family. Many people in my audiences were curious about how my involvement was affecting my family and home. Occasionally a woman would come up to me after a presentation and say, "I could never do something like that; my husband would never let me," or, "You must have a wonderful husband if he lets you run around like that."

Well, it was true I had a wonderful husband, but let me assure you that there is a price to pay for everything. He and I were slipping way behind in our relationship. Many feelings were being put on the shelf to wait for times that never came. Once, during a heated argument over my being gone so much, Dan said, "You've changed! You're not the girl I married!"

I knew he was right. I wasn't the same. Should I feel guilty? Should I try to change back? Is that even possible? What would God think of that? How did God expect me to follow him and still keep a marriage together? I'm sure Dan felt that he had lost me to another love. I could understand his feelings but I didn't know what to do about it. "God, I've trusted you with my life. Help me to trust you with the consequences."

My speaking continued for the next two years, averaging four talks a week. Some of them were morning meetings, some were luncheons. About twice a week I was gone in the evening. I tried to keep up with our social life so that I would be spending some time with Dan, which meant we bowled in the church bowling league, played bridge, attended a couples' group at the church, and took in an occasional movie. Obviously, I wasn't home very often.

By 1969, I had spoken to over two hundred groups and I had some real tests during that time. Tension seemed to be mounting in our marriage. I recall one time in particular. I was booked up for three months, and Dan was going through a difficult time on the job. He hadn't been feeling well physically, and he was lonely and depressed. He may have tried to share his feelings with me but if he did, I didn't "hear" them. Perhaps I had learned how not to hear things I was unable to respond to. We were living almost totally separate lives.

Chapter 7

Sore Throat

My speaking continued although I was getting irritated by sore throats. I'd had a lot of them lately but hadn't gone to the doctor since my calendar was so booked. This time it was terrible, like strep throat or, more accurately, like you feel after a tonsillectomy. It became difficult to swallow and my voice sounded hoarse.

I asked my prayer group to pray for me and tried to trust that I would be healed. Once I had decided to trust God, I felt as though I couldn't call the doctor or that would indicate a lack of faith. I kept thinking, "It will go away tomorrow," or, "I'll give it one more day." I studied my calendar and picked a date four weeks away, when my obligations let up a little, as the time to call a specialist if it hadn't gone away by then.

There were times when it was so sore and the laryngitis so bad that I had to touch a microphone to my lips and whisper to my audiences. Finally, I had no choice but to make an appointment sooner than I had planned. I was sure a specialist would simply give me a pill and perhaps suggest I rest my voice and I would quickly recover.

As I drove to the doctor I prayed, "Lord, you know I'm out there doing your work so you'd better fix this up or I'll have to quit." I really didn't have any great concern, just a sense of being inconvenienced.

I watched the doctor's face as he examined my throat. He probed and studied, probed and pressed. I watched his forehead wrinkle and the corners of his mouth drop as he finished his examination. Very seriously he shook his head, pushed away on his little stool, dropped his hands in his lap, and spoke. "Mrs. Zakich, I don't know if this is going to be hard for you or not since I don't know you and I don't know what you do. But I must tell you to go home and cancel everything on your calendar and announce to your family, and to anyone else who needs to know, that you cannot make a single sound for one month. I want to see you in thirty days, and I want nothing to come out of your mouth during that time." He added that if I accidentally spoke I'd have to start counting from that day. I was to begin the next morning.

I sat and stared. My body seemed numb. How on earth can I be silent for a month when my kids ask me two thousand questions a day, and the phone rings a hundred times a day, and I ask Dan seventy five questions a day...

I left the doctor's office to enter a new experience, a very different life style. One of complete silence. One that was to test my faith.

As I drove home, my world began to crumble. The first thing I thought about was the boys, ages nine and ten at the time. How could they get along without my guidance? My head began to spin with the things I always needed to say to them. "Brush your teeth, comb your hair, button your shirt, shut the door, don't let the dog out... where's your homework? And *please*, stop teasing your brother." How could I be a mother if I couldn't say those things?

My next thought was, "How can I be a *wife*? What sort of relationship will we have if I can't talk? Would we even have one?" Dan had never been very talkative to me. Would he tell me anything if I couldn't ask him?

Then my mind went to my calendar. Twenty-six speaking engagements spread out over the next three months. How could I get out of those? How I dreaded telling the program committees. Telling? I wouldn't be telling them anything. I would have to send letters – how impersonal.

One by one, thoughts came to me as to how this was going to affect my life. I was almost home when a lump in my throat blocked out the soreness and tenderness I'd been experiencing for weeks. I want to cry... but I don't cry, I thought. I hadn't cried for years. I prided myself for being so in control that I never fell apart. What was this strangling feeling in my throat?

I had been raised at a time and in a family where feelings were never expressed. Emotions were downplayed, at least the sad and negative ones. I remember as a child being told so many times, "Don't cry! Don't be a baby! Be a big girl." If I was hurt, someone would say, "Oh, that couldn't hurt!" If I felt sad, someone was right there to tell me it was foolish and that I'd get over it by tomorrow. If I was lonely or left out, I was told that I shouldn't feel that way, that I had lots of friends who just happened to be busy at the time. I was never allowed to be afraid or embarrassed or angry – not if I was a nice little girl. So I learned in my childhood that feelings were dumb. People weren't supposed to have them. And if they do, they certainly don't let everyone know. Now my eyes started to blur as the impact of a month of silence began to hit me. I felt as if a gallon of tears was waiting behind each eye, pressing against my eyelids, wanting to flow like Niagara Falls – but I couldn't let that happen. I might have an accident.

Oh, the frustration of arriving home to find unexpected guests visiting. *Why did they have to stop by on this evening?* I opened the front door and stood there, trying to throw all the necessary internal switches to turn me into the plastic person I had been most of my life. I certainly didn't want these casual friends to know I had emotions. Somehow I managed to bury my hurt and fear. When my husband asked, "What did the doctor say?" I calmly responded, "Oh, he told me not to talk for a month."

I wondered why the couple laughed, and then I could have sworn I saw a grin under Dan's beard. A strange emptiness swept through me. One of the men went over to Dan and said, "Congratulations. Where did you find that doctor? Maybe I can make an appointment for my wife!" Everyone burst into more laughter. *How could they joke at a time like this? Couldn't they sense that my world was crumbling? Didn't they care?*

I excused myself and raced into the bedroom, dreading having to return to that circus in the kitchen. Where were the sympathetic words? Where was the embrace and comforting words I so needed?

My next question was interrupted by the boys racing into the bedroom and asking what the doctor had said. Because they showed such interest, and because I'd been wounded by the others, I got down on my knees and said in a soft voice, "Children, come here. Mommy has something to tell you." They stopped dead in their tracks and they walked slowly toward me with serious looks on their faces.

I took their chins in my hands and said in a shaky voice, "Now you're going to have to be brave. It's bad news." Their eyes were big as saucers as they listened to me say that their mother wouldn't be allowed to talk for one month. Before I could finish telling them how we could get through it if we were all brave, they burst into a cheer, leaped into the air, grabbed each other, and ran from the room. The last words I heard them say were, "Yea! Let's go tell Jimmy and Donnie and Bruce and Stuart!"

After dinner that evening, I stood at the kitchen sink scouring a greasy skillet late at night as Dan made a list of things to do in the morning.

1. Call the phone company and have the phone disconnected.
2. Make a "Do Not Disturb" sign for the front door.
3. Call the relatives from work.
4. Buy a large chalkboard and a large box of chalk for Marilyn.

5. Go to the library and check out some books to read.

I wanted desperately to share my feelings with somebody but there didn't seem to be anyone around who was interested. Just when I started to say something, Dan announced that he was going to bed since he had to get up early. I stayed up and wrote a few notes before going to bed. Then I lay awake for hours feeling forsaken and forlorn. Morning eventually came and I was awakened by my sons running into the room to donate their crayons, tablets, and Mickey Mouse magic slate. Fortunately, they were old enough to read.

The silence began. The first days I felt challenged. I mentally put on warrior armor and set out to conquer. I've always been able to make a game out of the distasteful things in life in order to endure them. So that's what I did on my first silent day. I entered into the arena determined to be the best mute ever.

My fortitude lasted for a half day. While the boys were in school and Dan was at work, I wrote many notes and I made lists on the chalkboard. I looked out the window and watched for the mail. I listened to the radio, then watched an afternoon TV show (I had given up my soap operas). When the boys came home from school, they stuck their heads in the door and yelled, "Hi, Mom! We're going down to Jimmy's. Bye."

Hey, wait just a minute. I have some notes for you, I shouted in my head. *You can't play until you've done the chores I wrote on the chalkboard,* I yelled mentally as I saw them leaping over the juniper bushes in the yard. *No fair. I've waited for you all day.*

My sons quickly learned that never to look at the chalkboard was never to have any responsibility. Their posture actually changed. They began to walk around with their heads down so they never had to respond to my charades or the faces I would make as I mouthed my messages.

When Dan arrived at home from the office I experienced even more frustration. He always had a routine when he walked through the door and even this day was no exception. The door opened and he said, "Hi, Hon. I'm home." I raced into the room. Then he said,

"How'd it go today?" to which I shrugged my shoulders. I followed him to the bedroom where he ritualistically kicked off his shoes.

His next utterance came as he opened the closet door and looked at his sport shirts. "Where are the kids?" This time I had to push my way into the pants-section of the closet to go through the gestures of trying to communicate. "Down at Jimmy's?" "Was there any mail?" "What's for dinner?"

I realized in the days to come that those questions didn't require answers. They were his way of saying simply, "Hi, I'm home." When I stopped trying to gesture the answers, he didn't even notice.

Our family in 1969 - Dean, myself, Dan, and Darin.

The next few weeks I thought I was getting a glimpse of what hell must be like. I was in the world, but I couldn't participate. It was as if I was invisible. I couldn't affect anything. Everything began to irritate me. Noises, conversations, laughter, TV, being alone, watching the neighbors enjoying themselves chatting on the lawn, not being able to holler down the hall or respond when I heard the boys plotting some scheme.

One night, about the third week, it got the best of me. I couldn't sleep. The boys had bounced the basketball in the living room and broken my favorite figurine, a statue of a young girl

48

kneeling with her face turned up to God and her hands cupped in her lap. On the underside the caption read, "Here I am, Lord, send me." It was the crushing blow; the straw that made the load too heavy. Maybe it was the way my son reported it. "Hey, Mom. This guy's head fell off." I fell apart inside. *This is too hard, Lord! Why are you doing this to me? Did I do something wrong? Lord, are you there?*

I paced the floor until well after midnight. Frustration turned to anger. Red-hot anger. Every time I thought of God, the anger increased. Where was he in this? I just couldn't match it all up with God who had seemed so loving. The God who had been guiding me. I became enraged. *See if I ever do another thing for you!* I shouted in my mind. I went on to remind him of all the things I had done on his behalf in the last few years. *Lord, I went to the inner city for you and then was willing to speak to all those scary groups because I thought you wanted me to. This doesn't make sense! Now you take my voice from me! Why? Why?*

No response.

To scream so loud inside your head and not get any sign that it's been heard by anyone seemed devastating. I collapsed in a chair, exhausted and confused. I began to get in touch with the feeling that was down under the anger; the hurt at that huge rejection from God. *Where do you go when God rejects you?* I wondered. I decided that I'd have to put all thoughts of God out of my mind if I was to be able to go on. *Maybe he doesn't even exist. Maybe it's all in people's heads.* Whatever – it didn't matter now. I was never going to church again and I was never going to pray anymore.

I closed the door on God that night and went to bed without saying goodbye to the Companion I'd had through so many experiences.

Chapter 8

Surgery

The remainder of the month was mentally and emotionally painful. I stopped writing notes. I stopped smiling and doing my charades to communicate. I stopped looking for the mail every day. Nothing seemed to matter.

The furor inside continued to rage. When I saw people laughing or when someone said something and I couldn't respond, or when I saw Dan enjoying himself reading, I was enraged. It made me furious that none of my friends had the gumption to rip the Do Not Disturb sign off the door and say "Forget it! I want to see you!"

I learned some very interesting things about anger during my silence. One discovery was that anger is no "fun" at all if nobody knows you're mad. The few people I saw all seemed to think I wanted to be cheered up. They'd tell me jokes and clown around until I forced myself to respond. Inside, I didn't want to laugh. I wanted to cry.

Finally, on the thirtieth day of silence, I went to the doctor feeling proud inside that I hadn't said a single word. I walked into the treatment room expecting to be congratulated and praised. The doctor would marvel at the progress.

He sat down on his little rolling stool, took a tongue depressor and some sort of long scope, and began to investigate. I watched every face muscle and tried to interpret his changes of expression. I strained to see a reflection in his glasses of what he was seeing, but to no avail. Finally, after what seemed like an eternity, he spoke. "I'm afraid we're going to have to operate. I'll have Janice call the hospital and make arrangements. We'll try to get you in tomorrow morning and, of course, no talking beforehand." Everything inside of me went limp. There was a feeling of disbelief as I looked at him, the same feeling I'd had a month before.

My doctor, a wonderful man, did explain in his medical language what he was going to do, but instead of easing my mind, it caused ninety-six questions to form in my mind. Questions that would never be asked, let alone answered.

I was put in a hospital room with three other women who talked incessantly, each describing in gory detail her problem and the operation she was awaiting. One was going to have a tumor removed from her throat, and I wondered why she could talk and I wasn't allowed to. After asking me a series of probing questions that I couldn't answer, they gave up and left me alone.

The evening seemed long. I tried not to think. I tried not to feel. The TV was blaring and cigarette smoke was hovering over my bed. I stared out the hall to watch for any activity. Suddenly there appeared in the doorway a tall handsome priest, all in black. As I was wondering who he was, he asked which one of us was Mrs. Zakich. My heart skipped a beat. Who was he and how did he know me?

One of my roommates pointed to my bed. He walked over and ever so gently explained that he was the husband of one of my Episcopalian friends from my old prayer group. He had come to pray for me. Pray for me? I felt a rush of blood go to my head as I looked at the three women who had stopped talking and were now staring at us. *Why did I feel embarrassed? I wasn't familiar with Episcopalians. What did they do when they prayed?*

I want to shout, "I don't believe in God anymore," but my body just lay there. He asked, "Would you like me to pray for you?" I didn't know what that meant. Would he get down on his knees? Would he shout out loud? The woman next to me sat on the edge of her bed eagerly anticipating the show to begin.

I couldn't seem to shake my head Yes or No, so I shrugged my shoulders as though to say, "I don't care." What a shabby response, I thought, the moment I did it. A wave of humiliation swept through me and I felt immobilized and dumb.

He slowly reached out and put his hand on my throat. With his beautiful face toward heaven and his other hand raised as though to receive God's blessings, he began to pray aloud. "Lord, bless this special child of yours…"

"That proves it. He's got the wrong patient," I thought.

"Honor her faith, precious Lord, and heal her body…" His voice faded out when I began my own prayer: *"God, help him to hurry up, get done, and get out of here."* I was sweating as I peeked at the others, who had now turned down the TV. He finally finished his prayer, squeezed my hand, and said goodbye. With a sense of relief I covered my head and fell asleep, my only escape.

Morning came quickly and I was whisked off to surgery to have some tumor-like growths removed from my vocal cords. The shock of the operation was nothing compared to the surprise upon returning to my room to find the woman who'd had the throat tumor, sitting up in bed, smiling broadly. When she saw me, she blurted out, "Praise the Lord! I've been healed! Be sure to tell your priest friend when you see him that I prayed with him last night and asked God to heal me. When I was on the operating table this morning, the doctor said there was no tumor there. Isn't that wonderful? It was on the X-rays, but now it's healed. Thank you, Lord."

I felt bitter because I had gone through surgery, which meant that the prayer hadn't changed anything for me. I felt cheated. As the day went on, I thought about nothing else. I could see why it hadn't happened to me. I remembered that woman's interest, her eagerness to hear, her openness, her obvious faith. Somehow I had sabotaged myself. I was heartsick.

I left the hospital to go home to thirty more days of silence. I was tired of being angry and having no one notice. Tired of every day seeming the same. Tired of being tired. I became aware at this time that anger takes a tremendous amount of energy. Because I couldn't express the anger, it seemed to be eating me up inside. I felt empty. How can I go another month when I'm shriveling up and dying? I had hoped so much that I could contact all my old friends and my relatives after the first month and find out all the news. I had rehearsed things hundreds of times that I wanted to tell my family. The despair seemed incredible.

I entered my house to begin my new "sentence" with no ambition, no goals, no incentive, no interest. Just time, lots and lots of time. I didn't want to read or watch TV. I didn't want to be around Dan or the kids.

I retreated to our den which was located down a long hall, far removed from our kitchen and living room, which was the center of all activity. I became a hermit. I didn't want to think, feel, hear, or care about anything.

Self-pity became my enemy as it became more and more evident that the world, and certainly my husband and children, could get along quite well without me. In fact, it seemed as if my boys were happier than they'd ever been. Their quarrels were not as frequent. They were taking more responsibility than they ever had before. It was even evident that learning was taking place without my help or input. Oh, how my ego was suffering. The suspicion that nobody needed me kept me depressed and immobilized.

Chapter 9

More Surgery

Now that I've lived through that time of my life, I'm aware that some very funny things happened, though they didn't seem funny then. On the second or third day of my silence, I was sitting in a rocking chair looking out the window. Darin and Dean ran in from play shouting. "Mommy, Mommy, can we bring Jimmy and Billy and Donny and Stuart in? They want to look at you!" I thought, "Look at me?" But what could I say?

The screen door opened and in strolled a gang of little boys. They stood across the room and stared at me. What were they looking at? What did they expect to see? I realize now that it was probably the first time those kids ever saw me with my mouth shut.

And then something happened that was to be repeated many times in the weeks to come, with adults as well as children. They assumed that, because I couldn't talk, I couldn't hear. While I sat there, eight feet from them, one of them leaned over to another and said, "Does she still eat?" Another one said, "She looks funny, doesn't she?" When Jimmy asked my son if I *still went to the bathroom*, I'd had enough. I got up and left the room. As I walked toward the hall I heard a whisper, "Maybe she's going now!" When the screen door slammed five times, I knew they'd gone back out to play and I would no longer be on display.

We had a dog that liked to escape every time the front door opened a crack. One morning as the boys left for school, the dog made its getaway. I walked around the neighborhood for an hour and couldn't find her, and of course I couldn't ask for help. Later in the morning I spied her from the front window with three other dogs of varying sizes. I ran to the door, opened it, and realized that I couldn't call. I whistled my loudest high-school football game whistle. It worked. My dog came running, but so did the other three. In the door bounded what seemed like a wolf pack. How do you communicate with a batch of dogs when you can't make any sounds, and they won't look at you? I did everything I could; stomped my feet, made scary faces, clapped my hands, and waved a towel over them. The German shepherd thought I was playing and jumped into the air, grabbed onto the towel, and pulled me around the room until he won. It took a whole pack of wieners (I'd planned to cook for dinner) to lure three dogs out and one back in.

Another incident happened on a night when I hadn't prepared any dinner. Dan was so beautiful about being willing to take us out to eat if my day had been stressful.

That night we ate at a coffee shop a few miles from home. The boys chose a booth in the back and sat side by side while Dan and I took our places across from them. I took my tablet and pencil so I could participate somewhat in the conversation. As we waited for our food to come, I noticed my younger son's arm as he rested his chin on his hand. Streaks of dirt looked like they'd been there for quite some time. Would we ever get back to normal so I could remind them to take showers more often? I took my pencil and wrote, "Look at your arms. They're filthy. You MUST take a shower tonight." I handed it to him. He rolled his eyes in disgust and put the note down as our dinners were delivered to us. We had a lovely meal with very little strife.

As we were standing at the cashier's counter waiting to pay the bill, I glanced toward the back of the restaurant just in time to see our waitress pick up the note. She looked frantically at her arms, then shook her head in disbelief. Oh, no! She thinks I left that note for her. I turned and ran to the car, jumped in, and ducked down to the floor of the back seat. My husband, thinking I had gotten sick, rushed out and sped home.

Tablet and pencil did not seem to be an effective or adequate form of communication for me. At times, writing added to my frustration rather than eased it – partly because nobody waited around long enough for me to respond on paper to their questions. Everyone seemed to move so fast, to be in such a hurry. Public occasions were usually humiliating for me. Sometimes I would see a friend in the crowd and feel excited as she approached. "How are you doing?" she would say. "See you around." There I was, writing "Rotten" on my little tablet, then looking up to see that she'd gone.

Since I dreaded these public appearances by myself, I would cling to my husband's arm; he could explain that I couldn't talk. "How is she?" they would ask Dan, and he, knowing I was under the best medical care, would reply, "Oh, she's fine." Actually, I didn't feel fine at all! I was lonely, hurting, scared, cut off from life. The people might go on and ask if there was anything they could do, or did I need anything, and because Dan really did take good care of me the answer was, "Naw, she doesn't need anything. If she does, she writes it down and I get it for her." That was true, but I felt invisible because they hadn't looked at me so I could shake my head or nod or smile or frown.

One time I wished I *could* become invisible. I made the mistake of taking a note into the bank and handing it to the teller, who quickly pushed the silent alarm. Two men suddenly rushed up on either side of me. Security guards!

The realization that nobody really knew me began to penetrate. Some of my friends knew what I *thought* about a given thing, what my opinion was. But I had never shared my feelings with anyone. In a sense, I was completely alone. The real person I was, was living inside the robot that people had gotten acquainted with. The individual they knew wasn't really me, but rather was the accumulation of masks and messages I'd learned to show and give to be accepted. *How can I get out? How can I let someone in? It's lonely here!* Even my husband didn't know me, and it wasn't his fault. We'd spent almost all our time together discussing the kids, his job, and my social activities. We planned trips, balanced budgets, but didn't talk about our feelings.

Once when I was staring off into space in my rocking chair, my son came up to me, gently touched my face, and said in a soft voice, "Mommy, are you in there?"

~

The sixtieth day finally arrived, the first day in months that I was eager to get out of bed in the morning. I had watched the calendar and counted the days religiously, and could hardly wait to get to the doctor's office for my checkup.

I was led to a treatment room where I sat and waited, feeling smug. I did it! I did it! He'll see.

The doctor finally came in and did his usual probing and studying. I watched his forehead hoping to read the wrinkles, but they didn't match up with the slight smile on his lips. He said, "Your throat seems to be healing nicely. It looks like you've been very obedient about being quiet. I'll have my office call the hospital and arrange for surgery in the morning, so we can take care of the other side…" I couldn't believe it. I felt tricked. How could this be happening when I didn't know there were two sides to whatever he was doing in there! My heart sank. I can't do it, I thought. *I can't live through any more of this.* But none of these feelings found expression.

The next thing I knew I was entering the hospital with my little suitcase like an obedient child. Although I was in a room by myself this time, I still couldn't sleep. Fears began to creep in. *I bet I have cancer. I bet I'm dying and nobody is telling me.* Maybe that was why so many old friends had stopped coming around… because they all knew. I became paranoid. The nurses talking in the hall made me suspicious that secrets were being kept from me.

To whom could I turn? Who even knew that I felt troubled and scared? How alone I felt. I couldn't turn to God since I had written him off last month.

Two more growths were removed and I lived through it – much to my surprise. When the time came for dismissal, there was some delay with paperwork so Dan decided to wait in the car.

It was a beautiful sunny morning. The doctor insisted on accompanying me to the car, which was parked at the far end of the hospital parking lot. He put his arm around me and told me in a calm, soothing voice that everything seemed to go well and that I was a good patient. What *choice* did I have? I wondered what it would be like to kick and scream and pound and cuss, which is what part of me really wanted to do.

I suddenly became aware that he'd stopped. "Mrs. Zakich, I have something I want to say to you and I'm not quite sure how to say it," he said. My heart began to race. I felt my temperature begin to rise as I looked at him with my most questioning expression. "I don't want to frighten you but I do feel I should level with you. I hope you're not just sitting around the house waiting for this to be over (which is exactly what I'd been doing), since we won't really know much until after thirty more days of silence. Mrs. Zakich…"

My head felt like an echo chamber as I tried to focus my eyes. He looked down at his hands and then back to me, "I can't guarantee at this point that you'll ever get your voice back." My head began to spin. I leaned against a parked car and felt life slowly drain from my body. "I don't think there's anything to worry about, but I would suggest you give some thought to what you might do if you are a mute." *A mute? I can't be a mute! You can't do this to me!*

The doctor led me to the car and opened the door. There was Dan, patiently waiting while listening to the radio. He hadn't heard and I couldn't tell him. As he greeted me warmly and filled me in on everything the kids had done while I'd been gone, my mind was yelling, *"Thirty more days! Thirty more days! I may never talk again!"* I felt suspended in some strange time capsule. I couldn't hear, see, or think. My mind pushed a button that said "fast-forward" and I was frantically trying to see into the future.

I don't remember the drive home. I didn't have a tablet or a pencil so there was no way I could communicate what the doctor had said. Dan continued his report of everything he and the boys had done.

We arrived at the house and Dan was uncertain whether to go to work (it was ten-thirty in the morning) or to stay home with me. As we went in the front door he asked, "Do you need me to stay home or should I go to the office?" How do I answer that, I thought? "Well, what do you think? Do you feel OK?" *How can I tell him what I think or feel?* I stood motionless trying to assess my capabilities. I *really* was OK. I guess I don't really need him, I thought. I decided to nod yes to whatever he said next, and it was, "Well, then, should I go to work?" He gave me a kiss, said he'd be home at dinnertime as usual, and left.

Chapter 10

A New Creature

The moment the door closed, I was gripped by a wave of panic unlike anything I'd ever felt. Every cell in my body seemed electrified. The impact of what the doctor said hit me full blast. What my mind retained was, "You might never talk again." What it didn't remember was, "Now this isn't for certain. I just want you to be thinking about the possibility."

I remember running all through the house in a frenzy. It seems crazy, but I was beyond thinking rationally. I recall racing up and down the hall, looking in every room, opening doors, cupboards, drawers. In my mind I was shouting, *"What am I going to do? What am I going to do?"* I would think of my kids and every cell would scream, *I'm not done with my kids! I didn't tell them things that I need to tell them. O God, I'm not done yet!* Then I would recall some of the awful things I had shouted at them in the past. *O God, I owe them so many apologies.*

I thought of Dan and felt such remorse. How many times we'd talked about getting away by ourselves and talking, without any time schedules or interruptions. I longed to recapture the closeness we once had. Why had we put it off? It hurt to scream so loud inside myself. It was shattering to think that nobody could hear it – not even God, or so I thought.

The rest of the day I operated on "auto pilot." I couldn't sleep that night so I paced the floor until after midnight, asking myself questions, questions, and more questions. My thoughts turned to God and I wanted to cry. I knew I couldn't get through this by myself, but did I dare call on God?

I sat in the moonlight near my living room window and recalled the night I'd lashed out at God. I said I'd never pray again. I had shaken my fist at him and said, "Who needs you?" I felt sorry now, but I didn't know how to reestablish a relationship with him. *Would I have to beg to be forgiven? Should I offer to do something to earn his love? Would he help me after I'd been so nasty? Did he still love me after the way I'd closed the door on him?*

I realized I had no choice. I knew he was there and he was the only one who could lift me from this place and give my life meaning. I rehearsed what I was going to say to him. I decided to sort of bargain by saying, "All right God, if you give me back my voice, I'll never say anything bad and I'll never criticize my children again. Only loving things will come out of my mouth, Lord." I wondered if I could keep a bargain like that. I decided not to pray that one.

I got up and walked around for a while. Then I decided I needed to set up a "sanctuary" and get on with praying. I gathered some candles, a Bible, and a plaque with a picture of Jesus on it, and arranged them on the coffee table. In the back of my mind I knew I was just prolonging "getting on with it" by the rituals I was doing to get ready.

Something began to stir in me and my soul couldn't wait any longer. I said, *"O my God. O my God. Oh my God!"* Tears streamed down my face, my body began to tremble and sobs worked their way up from some place deep inside me. I crumbled to the floor and gripped the shag carpeting as waves of anguish flowed out of me. I had never cried so hard. I hadn't cried for thirty-five years. It seemed I was falling apart, never to be put back together again. I don't know how long I lay there, lost in my own pain.

There was no time in this realm, no awareness of the physical world, no phoniness, no intellectualizing, no cleverness. Just empty space, naked experience, and then – incredible awareness of the closeness of God. In that moment I knew he'd never left me. It was *I* who had gone from him.

I experienced God's forgiveness. I didn't have to grovel or plead for him to love me. He was enfolding and holding me in this desperate time. I felt such oneness with him as I poured out all those years' worth of tears, it was as though I was immersed in pure understanding.

I cried about the things happening and not happening in my life, about things that had happened prior to this time – in the inner city, and before that. My mind observed as my heart brought to my attention (and to God's) every hurtful or fearful thing that had happened in my life. As these experiences paraded through my consciousness, I was able to cry the tears that had waited so long for expression.

I told God that I didn't understand him. I'd felt rejected by him. I shared my doubts about having been led by him in my inner-city work. I cried about my marriage, my poor mothering, and my feelings of inadequacy. It was as though I was watching the pages on a calendar turn backward through my entire life, recalling everything that had made me want to cry: experiences in high school, losing the spelling bee in third grade.

With each new outpouring of tears I felt an outflow of energy until I was drained, spent, devoid of any power or strength. In the still space somewhere inside my hollowed-out being, a single thought winged its way. "*Did I die?*"

Tingles. I felt tingles in my hands, then in my feet. My heart began to beat noticeably faster as I admitted my excitement that I must still be alive.

With a sense of wonder and fascination, I experienced being filled with new life: something like warm honey flowing through every part of my body, liquid love being given in a transfusion, electric current coming into my body.

I had the desire to take a deep breath. When I inhaled, it was as though my muscles rejoiced in the peace that had come to them after what must have seemed a violent storm. Light. I felt filled with light, as if I was glowing. With my eyes closed, I could see myself filled with light, as if I was transparent. Light streamed out of every pore. I had such keen awareness in that moment of illuminated silence. I felt so alive, yet I wasn't moving. I felt so at one with God, and I wasn't even trying. I felt so at peace, and still none of my life's circumstances had changed. My mind felt uncluttered. There were no questions, no fears, no anger, no pain.

A prayer began to form in my mind, a simple, brief, uncomplicated prayer. *"God, what am I to do with my life?"* I felt it flow out of me, Godward, without any anxiety or effort.

A moment after that prayer-question, a thought seemed to enter me instead of flow out of me. My soul knew it was God. "I thought you gave your life to me."

I felt a bit of my old argumentative spirit awaken as I mentally defended myself. *"Lord, I did give myself to you. Remember at the retreat? Why do you think I went to the inner city? I was doing that for you. I did give myself to you."*

"If you've given your life to me, then why have you taken it back?"

That thought wasn't from me because I didn't even understand it. Had I taken my life back? My mind replayed my simple prayer, "What am I going to do with my life?" The words *I* and *my* seemed accentuated. I realized I had indeed taken responsibility for my life away from God. I longed for the relationship I'd once had with him. The trust that he would guide my life. The joy that came when we'd worked well together.

Very sheepishly I said, *"Lord, I admit I've taken my life back and I'm so sorry. I see now that I had begun to run here and there, schedule things without first checking with you, plan and organize as though I were alone, receiving all the glory for my accomplishments. O Father, forgive me. I want to offer myself to you, Lord, for whatever purpose you might have for a mute in Garden Grove."*

That night I gave up all my concerns I had about my kids and husband and I felt that a thousand-pound weight was lifted from my shoulders. I gave him my future and any career I might have. I promised to serve and praise him in all that I did from that day on.

I felt heard. I was immersed in his love, baptized by the tears of many years. Out of the silence came a word: *"Listen."* I was not to understand the significance until later. Right then I lay there and listened to the stillness, the night, the darkness.

I saw the image of a caterpillar crawling in the dirt, and then out on a limb. As though it were on a movie screen, I viewed a cocoon being formed. My heart fluttered as I realized the possible significance. I was in the cocoon of my life. I'd been in the dirt. I'd gone out on a limb. Now I was in a period when all seemed lost. The light had gone out of my life. I thought about the miraculous transformation that happens in a cocoon, and I got excited about the new creature that I was becoming as in my mind I saw a glorious butterfly emerge and take flight. I felt hope. *Oh God, thank you for the joy I feel. Thank you for revealing your resurrection power to me through a caterpillar. Lord, I patiently await the time when my cocoon cracks open and I fly free in you.*

I slowly got up from the floor, walked into the bedroom, crawled in bed, knowing that it had already happened. I had crawled into the arms of Jesus and was being rocked to sleep. Thank you, Lord.

The next morning I was awakened by my clock radio playing what seemed to be an unusually beautiful melody. I sat up and heard the boys in the kitchen (they had their own alarm clock since I couldn't tell them to get up), and their chattering sounded like music to my ears.

Dan emerged from the bathroom and began to get dressed for work. I noticed how handsome he was. His words of greeting seemed so gentle and loving, and I realized in that moment how much I loved him and how long it had been since I'd let him know it. How foolish to think that since I couldn't say it aloud, I couldn't express it in other ways. I wondered why I hadn't thought of that before.

I looked out the window and noticed that the trees looked greener. Then I heard a bird sing. What a gorgeous day. Why was it different... or was it?

For a while I honestly thought that everything around me had changed, but as the day progressed I knew for certain that it was I who had changed. I glided through the breakfast routine enjoying my children and their morning antics. There was tremendous optimism in me as I bid Dan and the boys goodbye as they went off to work and school.

I knew I was a new creature in Christ. This was the beginning of a new life.

Chapter 11

Self-Discovery

I walked through the house and wondered how it had gotten so dirty. I had tremendous energy and was eager to tackle long-neglected cleaning jobs. I hadn't felt like this in months. It was as though I was plugged into an inexhaustible source of power. I scrubbed, scoured, polished, and danced to the music I heard in my mind. *How can I be so enthusiastic and not know what I'm enthusiastic about?*

As the day wore on, I pondered what had happened to me the night before. I had experienced some magnificent change. Where were the worry and fear of the future? Where did the pain of the past go? It was as though I had been living my life in black and white and suddenly it burst into color.

Many times since, I have tried to figure out what happened to me. One night I saw an image in my mind of a jar of muddy water. It represented me. Over the years I had allowed people to pour all sorts of things into me. Opinions, ideas, information, prejudices, values, judgments. Add those things to a million unexpressed feelings and it all turns to bottled-up mud. I became afraid to share anything that was in me for fear it would come gushing out. I was certain that if anyone saw the real me he would never like me. So I was this jar of muddy water with the lid screwed on tight.

I was to discover that the same lid that held the stuff inside me kept me from being able to experience another person totally. The lid kept others from knowing me or loving me so that I could feel it.

As one might imagine, looking at the world through muddy water will distort everything. Hearing with mud in your ears makes for some strange messages and a lot of misunderstandings.

The more depressed I became with my throat problem, the weaker I felt – until I simply couldn't hold my lid on anymore. On that particular night, when I fell on my knees and cried out to God, my jar spilled. Out came all the contaminated water, right down to the sludge in my life. Out came everything that had been bottled up in me, everything that needed to be expressed, making room for God to pour his Living Water, his fresh, clear, Life-giving Water: Christ himself.

There was to be more silence, much time for meditating and contemplating, but it was a joyous time of rekindled love for God and my family. It was a time of hope. I constantly reminded myself that I was his, and that seemed to keep me from worrying. My faith seemed strong and I felt eager anticipation every day.

My third month of silence was unlike the first two months. This month was to become the most creative time in my life, a time of discovery and delight. I began to get acquainted with myself. To the degree, seemingly, that I could see and understand myself, I could empathize with and understand others. It was a wondrous time, when feelings became my friends as I learned to give expression rather than keep them prisoner in my body.

One of the first things I realized was that I'd have to get back out among people. Something inside me knew I was created to be with people, working, sharing, and serving. Initially, I would be embarrassed, but I would simply have to endure it until people got used to my silence. I began to venture out into the world again and to attend events. I returned to PTA and my church circle, my committees and our bowling league, our bridge club and my social clubs.

Now I was a spectator rather than an active participant. My pattern had always been to arrive early for a meeting, help set up, have a cup of coffee and chat with people as they arrived, organize things so the time together would run smoothly, and so on. Now I'd arrive as the meeting was starting so I could slip in unnoticed. I sat in the back so I could slip out without being questioned. I wanted to stay in the background since I couldn't contribute anything to the discussions or conversations. What a switch for a person who always before sat in the front row, had a comment for everything, and was always raising her hand.

I saw every one of those situations from a different perspective. Being in my old groups as a silent member was an experience that taught me many lessons.

As a constant spectator, I became a listener – not by choice but by default. I was surprised at what I began to notice as I focused my full attention on someone I thought I knew "like a book." I didn't really know the person at all. I learned that to really listen to someone you must give her your full attention (which I had never been willing to do before). You must observe her body language, look at his facial expressions and hand motions, and most important, try to *feel* his feelings. I'd never listened like that before because, when I had my voice, I was always rehearsing what I was going to say when someone was talking to me. I could hardly wait for the person to take a breath so I could interject *my* thoughts, ideas, opinions, what I'd read or seen on TV - whatever would build me up in the person's eyes.

Sensitivity to others was born into me at that time. I began to hear past the words people were saying to what they were trying to say. I desperately wanted to communicate with those around them, but I wasn't able to communicate even when I had a voice. I'd have to begin by writing my thoughts and messages even though I'd had many shattering times with my little notes not being read or understood. I knew quick jots would never suffice as a form of communication. I'd need to write at home, on all of the subjects that were important to me, and then find people to read them.

I hadn't realized how many hang-ups related to writing I had. My dread of writing showed up in my always being delinquent in letter writing, never making a grocery list even though Dan asked me to every week, and not liking to write excuses for the boys if they missed school.

In my silent meditations I traced this negative feeling about writing back to an experience in fifth grade. I was to write a report. I don't recall the subject, but I remember that ordinarily I copied something from a book, trying to reword it just enough to make the teacher think I'd understood what I was writing about. This time, however, I tried to write my own thoughts and feelings about the subject. I remember my excitement, thinking I had an understanding of what I was writing about. I put little philosophical comments in it, and I thought it was the best report I'd ever done. I carried it to school in a construction paper folder as if it were gold.

When I arrived in my classroom, I went to my seat and waited for a time when the teacher didn't seem too busy. I walked slowly up to her desk, placed the folder there, and returned to my seat. I watched her as she read it. I was nervous. Then devastated, I saw her frown, pick up her red pencil, and begin to make circles and checks all over it. She must not like my ideas. I must really be dumb, I thought.

I see in retrospect that I made a decision that day in fifth grade. I would never write my feelings again. I would never risk having someone read them and judge them by the spelling, punctuation, and whether or not I put a capital letter in the right place. It had affected my whole life. I had avoided writing ever since.

Now, however, since I had no voice, writing seemed the logical form of communication. Although it was hard to know where or how to start, I began. I wrote everything that came to mind. I poured out every thought, idea, and feeling on paper. I wrote about every emotion I could label. I wasn't writing for anyone to read, at first; I just wanted to get these things out of my body. It seemed that I could better understand and deal with things outside of myself than things inside. I wrote about frustrations, concerns, hopes, dreams, fears. I wrote prayers and even composed the answers I thought God would give. It was a beautiful release.

After several days of writing, I noticed that some of my thoughts had a rhythm to them, sort of like poetry. I'd written practically no poetry, but this seemed to flow out of me and I was fascinated as though it came from someone else. Such a time of self-discovery. I read and reread my compositions and poetry and was amazed at what I was learning about myself. One day, Dan bought me a big box of oil pastels and I started to express some of my inner reactions with colors. I scribbled, colored, designed, and smeared magnificent colors. I had a freedom I'd never had before. It was so good to know that no one was going to grade it or ask, "What's that?"

The hope that I could accomplish something in my life was being restored. It even occurred to me that some people communicate through music and, although I'd always loved music, I was not a musician. During those days I would find myself sitting down at the piano and plunking out a tune I was hearing in my head. Much to my surprise, I began to combine my poetry with music. I never knew these abilities were inside me, but they must have been there all my life. It seemed amazing I'd never discovered them before.

I realized the power of negative reinforcement, since I could see that that was the reason I had never tried these things after I got out of school. By that time I was pretty convinced that I was incapable and had no talent. When everyone around you says that something you've done is good, you soon start to believe them because they're the judges present, I was experiencing the joy of expressing myself and was loving every minute of it. It was as if every day was Christmas and I was finding gifts within myself and getting to open them one at a time.

So, my third month of silence became the most creative time of my life. It was such a contrast to the previous two months. When I wasn't home doing something creative, I was attending something and trying to listen creatively.

Every so often I would think about my experience with God that night. I would wonder what he meant by *"Listen,"* but maybe that's what I was doing. I was listening to myself and those around me in a completely new way.

71

Chapter 12

Learning to Listen

Day in and day out I listened to conversations between: husbands and wives, parents and kids, teens and friends, committee members, brothers and sisters, and I became increasingly horrified with what I was hearing. I no longer heard only the words. I now seemed able to hear past the words to people's trapped feelings.

I would come home from a meeting or social gathering with conversations being replayed over and over in my mind. I heard the echoes of a conversation between a couple we played bridge with. The wife had tried to share a feeling and the husband had reacted to her words and missed the point. He couldn't be blamed, though, because she had disguised her feelings by making a statement that made him feel a need to defend himself. She said, "Jim, we never do anything anymore." (I suspected she was wanting to say, "I miss your undivided attention.")

His reaction was to point out to her all the things they'd done together in the past month: grocery shopping, attending church, visiting her aunt, etc. He then reminded her that at the very moment they were playing bridge together and it was her bid. The rest of the group laughed, and I watched her crawl into a shell for the rest of the evening.

I grieved when I recalled a little four-year-old who wandered into the living room saying he'd heard a noise and couldn't sleep. He was told, "You'd better disappear before I blister your bottom!" I watched his little lower trip tremble as he hung his head and walked down the long hall alone. I wondered if he really wanted to say he was afraid, but had already learned that "big boys are supposed to be brave." So he made a statement that was not even heard. On top of his fear he now had to add the humiliation of hearing the adults laugh as his parent threatened him.

As I recalled such vignettes, I realized that everyone seemed to be talking in code and no one was taking time or had skills to decode the messages. Someone would say some words and someone else would react to those words. They're not saying what they mean or meaning what they say! How can they communicate that way?

I made a startling discovery about myself that night as I faced the fact that I was just like the people I was watching and listening to. I searched myself for clues as to how I got that way and how I could change. The discovery was that all my life I'd had a sarcastic sense of humor. I could cut somebody down in a flash with a few words and have everyone else laughing at the same time. I had felt powerful with that ability and had used it since high school. I could see how I'd used it recently with my husband and kids.

But why did I do it? Why did I always have to get a laugh even at the expense of another person? I could see how I even set up situations to slay someone in the presence of an audience. (I wasn't sarcastic or joking when talking to one person, but just when I had an audience.) I did a replay of some of those times in my life and could see now that, at those moments, I had been hurt or embarrassed or threatened. But I couldn't let anyone know, so I was like a wounded animal that snapped at those around me.

I didn't like looking back at those incidents but they gave me insights, not only into myself but into those I came in contact with every day. I began to see that everyone was probably hurting to some degree – was perhaps lonely, frustrated, feeling inadequate, but feeling the need to pretend that he or she had it all together and was doing great.

I prayed an ardent prayer that night. *"Dear God, how can I help people communicate more effectively? How can I help people get in touch with feelings that have been bottled up for years? How can I help others get feelings out of their body so they don't cause ailments? Lord, how can I help people break the codes? Or not have them speak in codes anymore? O God, help me to help them."*

In the days to come I began to notice how differently I was acting toward my children. It was such a contrast to the first month when I wanted to grab them and shake them, and the second month, when I almost didn't care they existed. I watched and listened to them with a sense of wonder, and had so much more patience than I'd had before. Because I was calm, I was able to hear more of what they were saying and, lo and behold, I started to be able to hear beyond *their* codes.

One day my son came home from school and barged through the front door. I looked up from my rocking chair in time to see the glass shake in the window. He threw his lunch box down, stomped his foot, and screamed, "I hate school! I'm never going back! My teacher's mean!" With that he stormed to his room and slammed the door with such force that the entire house rattled.

Had I been able to talk, my reaction probably would have been something like this. First, I would have yelled at him for throwing the door open and hitting the wall. Then I would have reminded him of the glass in it (all of which he knew and had been reminded of a hundred times). I would have then screamed about the lunch box that cost six dollars, and belittled him saying, "Don't you know that thermos is breakable?" When he stomped to his room, I would have said, "Now you quit acting like that or you're not going to the park!" When he said he didn't like his teacher, I probably would have said, "Why, your teacher is a lovely woman. I met her last week at PTA..." More than likely, I would have gone down the hall and hollered through the closed door, "And you are *too* going back to school, if I have to take you there myself!"

That's the way I used to react to my kids when they got mad or threw tantrums. You see, for some reason I couldn't tolerate their getting angry. It triggered such anger in me that I usually sent them to their room with some sarcastic remark and several threats.

Thank God I couldn't talk. I learned a priceless lesson about decoding my son's messages that day. Because my old patterns of behavior were being broken, I had to find a new way to react to that kind of outburst.

My first sensation was one of shock. Then I felt anger at his harsh words and his banging the door against the wall. I was furious when he threw the lunch box. And I must admit that when he left the room, still yelling, the thought of strangling him entered my mind. Because I didn't know how to express my reactions when things were happening so fast, I just sat and stared. Immobilized. After pacing around for a few minutes, I collapsed on the couch, baffled as to how to handle such behavior. I couldn't just ignore it.

While I was searching for some calculated reaction, he reappeared, looking sober. He slowly walked over and sat down next to me, and in two minutes he had his head buried in my lap. Like a volcanic eruption, he began to cry, "Mom, it is so awful. The kids all laughed when I gave my report. I was so embarrassed!" Since I couldn't speak, I put my arm around him – which I wouldn't normally have done because we would have been yelling at each other. He went on, "My teacher said I didn't study, and I did." Then the story he had tried to tell in code began to emerge. He had gotten up to give a report he'd worked on way into the night. He mispronounced a word and the teacher corrected him. He mispronounced it again and the kids laughed. He got nervous and forgot a whole section. The teacher then told him to start over and there was that dumb word again. This time the class howled and the teacher told him to sit down. He felt shattered and he cried, and of course the kids teased him. I felt the pain the little guy was feeling. Tears came to my eyes as I lived through his tale of woe with him.

I hadn't allowed my boys to express any negative feelings (I was the judge). So why was I surprised that they learned to code their messages? Thank goodness, now I wasn't able to talk him out of any of those feelings. Now he could trust me with the real stuff. I watched a miracle occur right before my eyes. As soon as he finished his account, he looking up, saw my tears, sat up tall, and said, "Can I have a cookie?" We hugged and he trotted off. I had never seen him recover from anything so quickly.

My ability to decode improved with each day and before long I could interpret almost any message in a second. For example, when my other son said, "I hate Bobby. I'm never going to play with him again!" I heard that he was angry at Bobby. I patted him as he told me what happened. Bobby had invited him to go somewhere. My son got ready and went out to the curb to wait. When Bobby and his mother drove by, it was obvious that Bobby had taken someone else. (I found out later that his mother had told Bobby he could invite one friend and he invited two.) I could feel my little boy's heartbreak and rejection.

Questions often drive kids away. Questions like, "What happened? What were you doing there? Why didn't you tell him...? How many times have I told you...?" Now I was finding I got all the information without asking a thing if I showed genuine interest and touched or held the boys.

The most profound experience of truly listening occurred when a young girl came to my house and pounded on the door for five solid minutes. I didn't always answer the door when I was home alone since I never figured out how to handle kids, or salesmen, or someone selling their religion. When I finally opened the door I saw a forlorn young woman whom I'd met only once. She was sobbing.

My first thought was, "Does she know I can't talk?" A wave of inadequacy swept through me as I tried to gesture to her that I was unable to speak, but she didn't even notice my hands waving around or my pointing. She stumbled in and went to the kitchen where she collapsed at the table and continued crying. I didn't know what to do, so I just walked around the kitchen and looked at her as she slumped over. I wasn't used to being around someone crying. I always felt so awkward if a person even got choked up, and I would do everything to change the subject, make them laugh, or pretend I didn't notice. None of those old patterns seemed like options in this case. *What can I do? She's hurting, Lord. What can I do?*

She eventually began to tell her story. "My dad kicked me out of the house. I hate my dad, he doesn't understand." She said it with such emotion that I felt what she was feeling in every cell of my body. She went on to say she'd been kicked out because her dad found out that she was pregnant. Her dad hated the boyfriend and had warned her that if she continued to see him she'd have to move out. "I don't have any place to go," she sobbed.

I tried to imagine what it would be like to be pregnant, unmarried, and have no place to go. I felt a heavy grief for her and wanted somehow to let her know. "Touch her," I said to myself. Why did that seem so hard? I never touched people. Still, it was the only way to get some people's attention if I needed to act something out. I remember looking at my hand and wondering why it felt like lead, why it didn't want to move. My mind said, "Do it!" but my body said, "I'm not used to this. What will she think? What if she pulls away?"

My mind won over my body, and I put my right hand on her shoulder. The most amazing calm came over her in the next few minutes as I just patted her. Her story continued with the painful discovery that her boyfriend now loved someone else and had broken up with her. She twisted and writhed as she told of the love and trust she had in him.

How I felt the pain of the lost love. My tears began to flow as I shifted from feeling the anger about her father to the grief of her loss. Her world had collapsed it seemed, but there was still more. Word of her pregnancy had spread through the place where she worked, and her boss had called her in and fired her from the only job she'd ever had. She pleaded with him to allow her to stay since she would have to get an apartment, but he hadn't been persuaded. Then she'd backed her car into a parked van in a parking lot, and, because her insurance had expired, she left the scene without reporting it. Now she was terrified of being caught.

I had never heard so many traumatic things come out of anyone's mouth at one time. Probably I had never listened to someone's whole story before. (Another realization about myself.) Had I had my voice, I would have done as I always did. At the end of their first sentence, I would start making suggestions, or wisecracks. Or I would use their opening line as a kickoff for one of my own stories, making it big and dramatic so they would think theirs was little in comparison.

What a sickening discovery. How many times had I said to someone, "Oh, don't worry about it, it'll be better tomorrow," or "So, who needs him?" "Tell him where to get off!" "You can find another job, there are lots of things available." How awful I'd been to people! I had never responded to their feelings. I hadn't even fully heard their complaints. My whole lifestyle was designed to shove feelings back and to act as if I never had them.

Here I was, allowing someone to get her entire painful experience out of her, and, much to my amazement, I was feeling what she was feeling. I continued to pat her as she went on unloading everything that came to mind. For the first time in my life I felt comfortable crying with someone. She must have known I was listening although at times she was so into her story that she seemed oblivious to my presence. Finally it was finished. She stopped crying and shaking. She looked up at me for the first time and I'm sure she noticed that my cheeks were wet with unwiped tears. I jumped to my feet, grabbed a box of Kleenex, offered her one, and we both laughed (hers was aloud, mine was silent). I felt led to offer her a cup of coffee, so I went to the stove and pointed to the coffee and also to my cup rack. She said, "Oh, I'd love one." As we looked at each other and smiled, I didn't realize I was witnessing a transformation of a human being.

Suddenly she said, "I suppose I could call Cindy and ask if I could stay there for a few days. I could probably get a job at Lamberts. Hey, and I could ride the bus there! I could babysit my sister's kids and start saving money…"

She began to talk faster, getting more excited with each possibility. To my amazement I realized that these thoughts were not coming from outside sources, they were coming from inside her. Soon she was standing up and saying, "Yeah, if I did ____, then ___ would probably happen and then I could ___." Her arms were flying in every direction as she enthusiastically dramatized the possibilities.

I was thrilled that ideas were coming to her, so I did everything I could to show it with my body and expressions and hands. We were both kind of dancing around the kitchen when all of a sudden she stopped. She looked directly at me for a second and then, like a rush of wind, threw her arms around me. "Oh, Marilyn, thank you, thank you!" I had never been hugged so tightly or sincerely. What had I done? I had never been thanked like that for any advice I ever gave! She stepped back with a radiant smile on her face. "I'll let you know how it all turns out," she said as she ran out the front door.

I was stunned. I watched her briskly leap over the shrubs surrounding the yard. She was gone. What had happened? What transformed that girl from a caterpillar to a butterfly? *Dear God, help me to understand how it happens so I can bring it about intentionally rather than just by accident. Lord, is this what you mean by listening? Am I doing it? I want this to happen in all my relationships.*

I spent hours pondering and meditating on that experience in the following months, searching for the secret of it. While it was happening, however, I was unaware of the impact it would have on my future. It was like watching a flower unfold, not really able to see it happening, but suddenly aware that it had. More than anything in life, I wanted to be able to facilitate more of that kind of life-changing experience. It became my dream and my prayer in the days to come. As I relived such experiences I began to get clues. The first clue was the similarity of what happened to her to what happened to me that night with God. That pouring-out of all that darkness and getting right down to the sludge of life in the bottom of the jar. Having it heard and accepted, not discussed or challenged or criticized. No advice was given.

The Holy Spirit had worked through me. I began to wonder if problems and solutions came in matched sets. Maybe we can't get in touch with our own solutions because they get covered up by so many people's advice and suggestions that they get buried.

When we lose touch with the creative part of us that "knows," we feel inadequate and insecure. This kind of listening could free people from the prisons that are built by us – first as a hiding place, but then becoming the only place in which we know how to function.

I had built a prison around me and then sat inside wondering why I had no visitors. *Oh God, help me take the walls of my prison down so I can be available to haul away the debris of someone else's life.* I knew I couldn't take anyone else's walls down, but I could wait outside, loving and encouraging someone while he did it.

Maybe I can become a professional "listener," I thought. Maybe that's how God is going to use my life. I had listened to that young girl with my whole being, not just my physical ears. Maybe that's what is meant when people talk about listening with the heart. On that occasion my mind was not filled with rehearsing, planning, staging, or worrying about how I would come across. The result was that she and I felt a communion, a closeness. She knew it and she felt freed.

Chapter 13

The Road of Life

My head seemed full of discoveries and insights. My heart felt tender and committed to finding some way to help people communicate. My body still felt energized even though it had been three weeks since my new beginning.

One night I prayed, *"Dear God, help me to find some way to use the things I'm learning, so I can help other people. Help me to pull together the bits and pieces of wisdom and truth and to put them into a form that can communicate. Lord, I need a way to reach out and touch the hurting people in the world. Speak to me tonight. Express through me tonight. O Father, show me how I might love in a way that heals others. Amen."*

I sat there at the kitchen table, pencil in hand, and waited for the Spirit to guide me. I had a large sketch pad in front of me, as I often did while I was thinking. I was in the habit of doodling as ideas came to me. Sometimes I would draw or make designs, other times I would write words or music.

On this night, I saw an image of people walking along a path going up a mountain. There were many on the same path, but each on a different part of the path. There were beautiful scenes of nature along with challenging landscapes. In order to get to the top of the mountain, each would have to pass through the various areas, but perhaps at different times. I could see other paths also, but they too, made their way through a variety of terrains.

Because people were spread out, they were experiencing the area they were in, alone, not knowing that someone had been there before them and that someone would be coming to the place after they had passed through. It occurred to me that maybe we are at different places in our lives from those around us. Perhaps that's why it's hard to find relationships or companionship at the deeper levels of our lives. Oh, if we could just tarry for a while at one of the resting places and be willing to share with someone else who comes along, letting that person know that we, too, have experienced fear in those dangerous places. If we could let another know that we get angry with ourselves when we stumble or lose our way, then maybe we could give encouragement. This might help one who is tiring or wanting to give up in despair.

We see others along the trail and assume they have it all together. We think they don't have any problems so we think, "How could they ever understand my problem?" I remember thinking so many times in my life that I had it harder than anyone else and that God must not love me as much. Now in my mind I could see that no one was exempt from trials and feelings like fear, grief, loneliness, frustration, anger, and so on. Yet people reacted in many different ways to the same obstacle. What made the difference?

As I was thinking about these things, I began to sketch a road around the border of the large tablet. I thought of it as the Road of Life. Next I drew things along the road to symbolize some of the feelings one might have on the Road of Life. I wrote Happy Times, Sad Times, Excited Times, and Depressed Times. There were places for loneliness, fear, joy, love, grief, and pride. I drew little way-stations along the road to represent the times when there wasn't any particular problem or feeling.

Could I ever get a group of people together to talk about where they are (and have been) on their path? I felt ecstatic at the thought until I realized that it wouldn't be easy to get them to talk about feelings if they had never expressed them before.

My hands kept working as though they were not connected to my mind, adding things here and there. I was watching my hands create something that I had to ponder in order to understand. Some of it I didn't understand. The road went around the board and connected so that it was unending. It occurred to me that we don't go through these areas only once in our life, but many times. Each time is different, depending on other circumstances and perhaps because we have a deeper level of understanding.

I imagined a group of my friends sitting around the table with my tablet lying in the center. All I had to do is get them to talk but none of them would. I asked them why they didn't want to share and they all answered at the same time with words like "criticism", "put down", "fear of being laughed at", "fear of sarcasm", and "belittling." They didn't want advice or a lecture. They didn't want to be challenged or have to defend themselves. And no joking.

It dawned on me that these were the reasons I'd never shared what was inside of me. The reason people could now share such things with me was because I couldn't do any of those things to them. I can't describe the feeling of elation I had when that all clicked!

Then I thought "How can I ensure that no one experiences those painful things?" I had no sooner posed the question than the answer came. Only one person should speak at a time. That would do it if I could get a group of people to promise to be silent while others talked about their life experiences and ideas. If they would be willing to do it, they might discover how different that kind of listening is and hear beyond the words to real meaning.

I saw my hand write across the tablet, "Everyone must be silent except on his own turn." Turn? I hadn't thought about turns, but I could see that there would need to be turn-taking. I marked the road off so dice could determine which area a person would talk about. I wasn't certain how to keep the group on the subject of feelings, instead of talking about baseball scores, politics, fashions, and their children.

After a while I put the drawing aside, but the scene continued in my mind as I took a small tablet and relaxed in the living room. I began to think of questions that might help people to share some of their inner self. Once I started to write them down, they just bubbled out. Some of them were questions I had wanted to ask someone. Others were questions I wished someone would ask me – and wait long enough for me to write my answer. Questions poured out of me long into the night, until I had nearly a hundred on many different subjects.

What four things are most important in your life? Share a turning point in your life. What do you want to be doing in ten years? If you were told you had only one week to live, how would you spend it? What is something that makes you angry? Share something that you fear.

I wrote several questions pertaining to childhood because I was discovering how connected we are to the child we once were. I am the sum total of every experience I had when I was little and, although my childhood was a hundred times better than some, I still managed to get bumped, bruised, and scarred emotionally. In more recent years I have found the tremendous value of sharing about those little (or big) childhood traumas with someone. I get rid of more sediment in the bottom of my jar. I feel a bit more whole. And after I've shared with someone about a painful childhood time, my response to things happening is different, and so is the degree of pain or sadness.

At some point that night I felt emptied and decided to go to bed. I placed the little tablet with the questions on the big tablet with the road. Somehow I felt complete. Something was finished. I didn't understand what happened. Would I ever be able to find anyone to sit around my drawing and answer my questions? Maybe I will ask my family. Maybe I'll just wait and see… I drifted off to sleep. I don't remember if I dreamed that night, but I do know that I never dreamed that those scribbles were going to change millions of peoples' lives.

A day went by before my family questioned it. They were used to seeing my artwork, scribbles, "interesting" clay sculptures, and wooden plaques, so they didn't always question things. Eventually, however, someone asked what it was. I grabbed my pencil and pad and wrote, "I think it's a game." My family offered to try it out that evening and I felt nervous. I found four spools of thread in my sewing basket to use for markers and borrowed dice from another game.

That evening we sat around the table and experienced my creation. More than that, we experienced each other as we played together. It seemed incredible, but we learned more about each other in one hour than we'd learned in five years. We had a marvelous time talking about things that had never come up in our conversations before. Things we were feeling or going through. Dreams we had. Our hope for the future, and so on. One brother sighed after a turn and said he was so relieved that the other brother hadn't laughed at what he said. Dan shared some fears he had about losing his job and we were surprised.

Finally, I could write about the things going on inside me and someone would wait until I finished. They cared. They were surprised at my being so lonely. It felt good to let them know I had feared having cancer or that I was dying.

Dan and I were shocked with an answer one of the boys gave to the question, "If you could have two famous people for parents, whom would you choose?" He thought for about five seconds and said, "Abraham Lincoln for my dad and Raquel Welsh for my mother." Dan and I looked at each other with big eyes. Since we couldn't talk right then, we had to remain silent. But I had included a few blank cards in with the questions that allow a person to ask someone a question or make a comment. So Dan used a blank card to ask our son why these two. Our son answered, "Well, we are studying Abraham Lincoln in class and I like him, and the guys across the street always talk about Raquel, so I thought it would be neat to say she was my mother!" We breathed a sigh of relief – for a moment we feared our little boy had grown up without our noticing it.

We had some laughs that night and we had some tears. There were several startling revelations. One in particular was when our ten-year-old drew the question, "What do you want to be doing in ten years?" He read it aloud and sat there staring for a moment. He flipped the card back onto the table, learned back in his chair, and said, "Ah, forget it! I'll be dead!" I was shocked. Why would my son say that? A few turns later someone could ask him about it and his response was, "Well, when I'm eighteen I'll have to go to the Vietnam War and I'll probably get killed." With that he pushed back from the table and walked away with his head down.

I had never realized that my children walked around with that cloud over their life. It was true the Vietnam War was raging and had been for as long as they could remember. It was on the news every night. We explored this for weeks and it was good. I was glad to be in touch with my boys' fears and concerns. It enabled me to comfort them, but most importantly, to listen to them. After his feelings came out and were heard, my son was able to hear our thoughts about the possibility that the war wouldn't go on forever. For a child who had never known peace, this was new to him. And even if it did, he wouldn't necessarily have to participate. Just hearing us say that seemed to relieve his mind. We saw positive changes in his attitude, schoolwork, and happiness. How happy we were to have uncovered that fear, so that he could express it and be comforted.

Together as a family we decided to christen the game, *Tell It Like It Is*, which was a popular phrase in those days, and it described exactly what we were doing for the first time in our lives.

Chapter 14

The First Order

A few days after our family had tried out *Tell It Like It Is*, we had guests come to our home for an evening. Since I was unable to talk, we had done almost no entertaining. People seemed uncomfortable around me since two-way conversations weren't possible. Most people would ask questions and then become embarrassed because they couldn't think of anything to say when I couldn't answer. Often I was exhausted after guests left, from having to play charades all evening. On this particular night Dan began the evening by saying, "Why don't we play this little game Marilyn made? We had a great time with it the other night."

We had known these friends for years, but we found we didn't *really* know them. We had played bridge with them, bowled with them, and had hours of enjoyable times together, but we never knew what was going on inside them. We laughed and they were able to share some of their pain. One of them was able to squeeze my arm and say, "I'm sorry I haven't been a better friend while you're going through this throat thing. I just haven't known what to do." That felt so good to me; to have someone say it out loud rather than act as if it would never occur to her that I might miss my friends.

After our beautiful experience together, the couple asked if they could borrow the game so they could play it with their teenagers. They went out the door marveling at things they'd learned about each other. The last thing I heard as they walked to the curb was, "We've been married twenty-two years. How come I didn't know that about you?" They both laughed and got into their car. I could hardly wait to hear how it went with their teens who they described as very quiet.

It was two days before my friend came to my door to report on their experience. Both of the kids had agreed to play for half an hour, if they could quit then. It was the first time in over a year that the four of them had sat down together, let alone said anything meaningful to each other. The father had been able to confess his feeling of inadequacy in knowing how to talk to or help his kids. Everyone listened. On the next turn the daughter got a card that said, "Name someone you respect and tell why." She immediately said, "My dad, because he's the most honest and generous man I know." There was a warm feeling in the group as the younger son was able to share how much he hated being compared to his older sister, and how he always felt put down by her comments. She reached over, touched him, and said, "I'm sorry." Everyone promised to try to be more sensitive to that in the future, and after an hour and a half they put it away and all hugged each other for the first time in years.

"I hope you don't mind," my friend says, "but my daughter took your game to school yesterday where they played it in one of her classes, and tonight she wants to take it to her youth group. She promises to bring it to you tomorrow. Oh, by the way, her teacher would like for you to make five copies for her classroom and I would like two or three for gifts." I was so excited that I danced around right there in front of her. Then it hit me. Seven or eight games? That single game took me all night to make. I couldn't imagine how I'd ever get them done, but I nodded my head anyway.

When her daughter returned the game the next day, she told me that what she liked most about it was that she could say something to her folks and not get a lecture or a lot of advice in return. Also, she could hear her parents say something without feeling defensive or blamed. "It's neat," she said as she turned to go. "I'll probably need to borrow it again."

I had my assignment – eight games. I didn't like calling it a game, though, because it wasn't a game. Games are competitive, and this experience wasn't. In games you play to win. In this, you play for the joy of playing. Games are usually pretend and in *Tell It*

Like It Is, it's just the opposite. You don't pretend; you try to be real. Still, it did have a board, markers, dice, and a deck of cards, all the ingredients of a standard game. I called it a game because there wasn't a better word to describe it.

In the coming days I was very busy drawing roads, typing questions on recipe cards, coloring pictures, writing captions, and composing rules. All the while I was praising God for what I could see happening in people's lives as a result of this simple tool. *"O dear Lord, thank you, thank you. This is changing lives already. Lord how can it be? Is this what you want me to do? I'll keep doing it until you let me know otherwise. OK, Lord? Thank you for the joy I feel as I make these games."*

I was to spend many hours at my kitchen table creating duplicates of my original. I began to get orders in the mail and with each order there was always a note telling me about an experience that someone had. My heart would sing. What a wonderful feeling to know that God is using you.

Chapter 15

I Can Talk!

One day, I saw on my calendar that it was the twenty-ninth day. Tomorrow I had an appointment with the doctor. I couldn't believe how fast the time had gone, compared with the other months. As I was coloring one of my game boards, I thought, *"You know, if I go to the doctor tomorrow and he tells me I'm going to be a mute, I think I'll be able to handle it."* I had discovered that, if I was open, God could use me and work through me in ways I never would have imagined. I had been finding someone to play the game with every day and, because of that, my mind stayed clear and empty of worry and concern. There were no bottled-up feelings. I felt attuned to God, keenly aware of his presence and of those around me. I could function this way and have a beautiful life, more beautiful than the life I had known before.

When I went to bed that night I prayed again. *"Lord, I'm beginning to think you have a purpose for this whole thing. I love what is happening in my life and in the lives of those around me, so I have to trust you, Lord. If you want me quiet for a short time or forever, I want to serve you. I can see you working in my life. I can feel you working in my life. I can feel your love. I yield to whatever purpose you have for me and I trust you with my life, even if I have no voice."*

I am confident that my healing began at the moment of my accepting God's will for my life. I felt healthy and whole that night, as though everything in me was in harmony and balance with the entire universe. I believe the releasing of what was bottled up in me (which I am convinced was the source of my throat problems), and the infilling of the Spirit of God into my life to a greater degree than ever before is what healed me.

When the doctor examined my throat, he had some of the same wrinkles on his forehead, but this time they were from disbelief. He couldn't figure out how he had made such a mistake. When he finished, he said, "Mrs. Zakich, I certainly hope I didn't worry you with what I said." I gave him a blank stare and waited for him to continue. "Mrs. Zakich, your throat has healed perfectly and I think it's all over. You should be able to talk now."

I couldn't think of one thing to say. I continued to stare, almost afraid to believe it. The doctor continued, "Your vocal cords have some scar tissue on them so you may sound a little husky for a while. You may need to have some voice therapy, but everything looks fine. You may not want to talk now, but just know that whenever you want to, you can begin again."

Everything was spinning. I felt lightheaded as I floated out of the office to my parked car. "*I can talk! I can talk!*" I shouted in my mind.

It felt strange to get into the car and begin my drive home on the freeway, alone, without anyone to tell. It was a while before I opened my mouth and heard my new voice. As I drove into our driveway, I paused for a moment to collect myself. *"O Father, don't let me forget what I have learned. I need you again, this time to help me reenter the mainstream of life. Help me to do it wisely."*

I started out with a whisper, but each day my voice grew stronger. It was glorious to be able to talk to my family, but I wasn't so eager to spread the word to those outside my family circle. At first I couldn't figure out why. It seemed strange to realize that I could now talk to all my friends and have to admit that our relationships were better and more fulfilling than before. Did I want to risk blowing it?

I feared we would go back to the old way of relating, with all the superficial chitchat and joking. I didn't want to return to spending endless hours on the phone talking about people and family problems. I didn't feel a great need to tell everything that had gone on in my mind during the three months. I prayed over and over for God to show me how I could use this experience in my new life, whatever style it took.

I began to search for a new purpose. I began to notice ads in the newspaper and mass mailings like the Penny Saver, for lectures, classes, and groups that talked about the things my church wasn't talking about. Dream interpretation, healing, prophesy, angels, casting out demons, and more. I wanted to learn how to pray, and the prayers I heard at church were usually asking God to do things. I wanted to hear from God like people in the Bible did.

The mainline church I attended did not seem to talk much about Jesus even though they quoted scripture and told *about* him. Their emphasis was more on God and social justice.

I began attending classes, lectures, and groups that had interesting speakers. I found a New Age center where I felt strangely at home with the other seekers. This group talked about Jesus like they knew him personally. I met people who could see auras and tell things they couldn't know except through some supernatural power. I talked with people who had near death experiences and some who had encounters with angels. I was especially fascinated by people who spoke in tongues. I saw miracles of healing and felt a loving connection with fellow seekers.

I met people who had conversations with Jesus like he was present to them, and not just an historical figure. I listened to astrologists. All the while I was reading my new Bible and finding places where people in Bible times did those things. I learned the Wise Men, also called Kings, were actually astrologers (Magi), and I wondered why my church friends frowned and shook their heads when I'd mention these things.

They would say with frowns on their faces, "That's New Age." They'd never tell me what that meant, but I could tell they thought it was bad. The love and acceptance I felt in the New Age groups was so different from the negative attitudes I encountered at church. That drove me to seek God in the fringe places: back rooms, houses, rented halls, and campsites.

It is my belief that the church (in the broadest sense) is responsible for the New Age movement, since almost everyone I met in these places had attended churches, but had questions their churches weren't addressing. So they searched to find others like themselves who were interested in discussing and experiencing what the Bible talked about. It made me wonder what the church was afraid of.

I had never sat in silence in my church – waiting for (and expecting) God to speak to me personally. But these groups spent much time in silence. I remember flickering candles, incense, and soft music playing that helped me forget the world and all its busyness. I remember feeling as though I was being lifted up to heaven where I was given new understanding about things. These groups didn't preach, they demonstrated and invited us to experience something. That's how I learn.

In the New Age group I found, I remember being led in a guided meditation where we were to see ourselves on the seashore on a beautiful day. After a period of silence, the leader said, "Now see Jesus walking toward you." I've always had the ability to imagine things, so it was easy to see the figure of a man coming toward me. Then the leader said, "Listen to what he has to say to you." When he got closer I felt a strong 'gush' of love flowing between us. He called me *Rhea* as we embraced. (I had never heard that name before, I'd always been Marilyn).

I knew in an instant that I *knew* him. I knew his Spirit. It was the Spirit that had guided me in all my trips to Los Angeles. No other words were exchanged between us, but the connection and love I felt changed me. When I left the meeting, I felt energized and hopeful, but didn't know why.

I didn't tell anyone about the experience. It seemed too intimate and too difficult to explain. But I carried the memory in my heart and found myself talking to this familiar Presence that now had a name, 'Jesus.' I began to tell people to call me Rhea. I felt like a new person so I wanted a new name. Someone told me the name Rhea means "flowing stream" in Greek. I didn't care if it was true (which it is), but I knew that something in me changed. I felt like I was flowing again.

I made more games and got more and more enthusiastic as I received letters from people requesting them. Some went to schoolteachers, some to psychologists, and some to ministers and youth leaders. Many went to families who wanted to improve communication at home. What a joy to walk to the mailbox each day and find letters sharing positive change in people's lives.

Chapter 16

I Quit

In a matter of weeks, however, I began to feel burdened by the number of game requests coming in. I was forced to work way into the night to complete them. It got so I put off going to the mailbox for fear there would be more orders and then I would be even more behind. *"Lord, why do I always feel tricked? Things start out slowly and I think they're blessings. Then they get bigger and bigger and I never know how to keep them under control. I'm afraid they'll engulf me. Help, Lord!"*

It began to take all my time, around the clock. I didn't know how to refuse or how to decide whom to turn down – partly because I was so ecstatic that I had found such a wonderful way to minister to people. I knew the need was so great, and I also liked the glory of getting letters that affirmed me in ways I'd never been affirmed before.

How could I get someone else to make the games for me? Maybe I could get a game company to pay me for the idea and just turn it over to them. I had to learn a whole new vocabulary in order to even think of things like that. I had never used the words: produce, manufacture, copyright, market, or vendors before. (None of these words ever appeared in a Betty Crocker cookbook.)

I wrote personal letters to toy companies and sometimes sent a sample or a detailed picture of the game. It took me ten days to write all the letters to the companies. And one by one, if the company responded at all, I got rejection letters. Each one was like the teacher grading my paper with a red pencil. "No one would be interested in a noncompetitive game," and, "Whoever heard of a game where people talk about feelings? People don't want to do that." "It doesn't sound fun and that's what sells."

So I still had nearly a hundred game orders and only twenty-four hours in a day. Many of my friends encouraged me to start my own company and produce the games myself. I didn't know the first thing about how to start. Where do you buy all the markers, printed decks of cards, boxes, and other supplies? I'd been delivering the homemade games in brown grocery bags. I didn't even know where to buy dice.

The next few months were as exasperating, humiliating, and exhausting as my three-month mute period. I spent days trying to understand language that didn't seem like English. Patent attorneys, printers, box manufacturers, plastic companies, loan companies. Nobody wanted my business because I only wanted to make a hundred the first time. Dan had been laid off his job and we couldn't afford any more expenses.

It got so I hated to go out with my little game board. I hated to make phone calls because I could never seem to explain my problem over the phone. At the end of one particularly frustrating day, I put my few samples under my bed, stuffed the unfilled orders into my kitchen drawer, and decided to forget it.

~

A year went by. I tried hard to put the whole thing out of my mind. If I received a letter, I thought, "It's nice that the games I used to make are helping people." I began to build a wall around my heart again, because I didn't know how to deal with this. I didn't know where God fit in. I was afraid to ask, for fear he wanted me to learn about the business world. I wanted nothing to do with it.

I began to pretend that I had forgotten about God, probably inwardly feeling that he'd forgotten about me. I didn't pray anymore. I couldn't allow myself to feel, because too many things had built up. I was uncomfortable if I saw someone who'd ordered a game four months before and wondered where it was. I didn't know how to tell them why I quit the game business. Dan was off work for the entire year, so I couldn't afford to buy the supplies even if I had wanted to. I felt guilty about the money I had spent so freely to keep everyone supplied with games for so long since I never asked for reimbursement.

I felt plastic again. How did I lapse into the old person I'd been? It happened gradually as feelings built up in me that I didn't share. I was all bottled-up again. I was unable to feel anything or relate to another person's problems. I didn't feel love coming in or going out. None of my friends or relatives had understood the things I was trying to do to get the game produced, but that hadn't kept them from constantly giving me advice. Everybody was telling me how to run my business, but they were never there with help or money when I needed them. I had to shut down.

One Sunday a friend came up to me at church and invited me to attend a class in her place. It was an eight-week course in parent/child relationships offered by a psychologist, and her tuition had already been paid. I had the time, and I felt the relationships around the house could use some strengthening.

I went to the class and found out on the first day that it was made up of school psychologists, social workers, and counselors. I was embarrassed when they asked me to share my name and occupation. I felt out of place so I sat in the last row each week and never said anything the entire eight weeks.

However, I loved what the class was teaching. In fact, it seemed strangely familiar, as if I had heard this stuff before. We learned how to communicate effectively. We learned listening skills and how to verbalize a message without using code. When the instructor stressed the importance of labeling and expressing feelings, I knew where I had learned it: during my silence. The course verified many of my own discoveries.

Near the end of the eight weeks the instructor asked if we felt ready to start our own classes. There was an interesting discussion about how to get a group together and how to break the ice so that people would share with each other. Everyone agreed the first class was the most challenging.

Then a woman suggested, "There ought to be a game or something that could do it." Inside my head I yelled, *"There is a game that can do that!"* But it never came out of my mouth until after class when I waited around for everyone to leave so I could talk to the teacher alone. I introduced myself and beat around the bush for several minutes. Then I said, "You know, I've made a simple little game. It's sort of dumb, but it seems to work for some people. It gets them talking about their feelings. It's nothing special, just some questions and this board with some pictures and stuff on it." I heard myself downplaying it as though I was preparing myself in case she patted me on the head and said, "That's nice."

To my surprise, she said, "Why don't you bring it to class next week and explain it? Maybe others would like to get one."

I went home with mixed emotions. Sort of excited. Kind of scared. Feeling a need to be cautious so as not to get hurt again.

I dug a game out from under my bed, dusted it off, and took it to the final class the following week. The instructor, Mrs. Rivet, called on me. I was relieved she hadn't forgotten. I placed the game board on the floor in front of the class. I didn't look up the entire time of my detailed explanation of the hows and whys of *Tell It Like It Is*. My little pictures on the board looked so childish. The lines making up the road were so wiggly.

When I finished there wasn't a sound. I eventually looked up and the class was just staring at me. Someone broke the silence with, "Where can we get one of these?" Someone else said, "Yes, I'd like several." "Me too." "Send around a clipboard so we can sign up." "When will they be ready?"

I went home with forty orders, which I added to the orders in my kitchen drawer. Now I really had problems. (Keep in mind, this was before computers, Kinkos, Staples… convenient copy centers were not yet just a five-minute drive away.)

The next day I called the instructor and asked if I could talk to her. She invited me to her home and I was there within twenty minutes. I felt foolish as I walked up to her door. I didn't really know what I wanted to talk to her about except that I needed help. It helped me to relax when she told me to call her "Betts" and fixed me a cup of coffee.

She let me pour out all my frustrations about the business world before she said, "Rhea, I'll go with you! We've got to get this game produced. There's a need for it. I can see it, and all the people in the class could see it last night. Let's just go do it!"

So we proceeded to go all over town exploring and examining possibilities. She had an energetic and optimistic spirit that nurtured my tired withdrawn one. We talked to all kinds of people and were given leads. We went places I would never have thought of.

Printed game boards at Goodwill.

Eventually we ended up at Goodwill Industries and visited the print shop where handicapped people learned the art of typesetting and printing. We talked to the head of the print shop and he said they'd never done anything like a game before. "But letterheads and envelopes do seem to get boring for the students. Maybe they could use a challenge like this." Hooray!" I thought. "We're in business."

"OK, Lord, it looks like the game is going to happen now… if I can afford the supplies. Help me, Lord, to know where the money is going to come from."

Chapter 17

Disaster

I continued to follow the leads Betts and I were given and make phone calls, trying to find the best prices for the parts we needed. Then a strange thing happened. Someone had given me the name of a man who worked at a cardboard company with the suggestion that he might be able to help us. There was only one problem - that person didn't know how to reach him. His name was Jim Hayes, and there were at least twenty people named Jim Hayes in the phone book. It wasn't fun to call down the list and ask whoever answered if the man of the house made cardboard boxes. Some people thought I joking, others simply said "No" and hung up.

Then the miracle happened. I had one more name to call and I was getting tired and depressed. I dialed a number and reached a woman who informed me I had the wrong number when I asked for a Jim Hayes. Then she said, "Wait a minute. Did you say Jim Hayes?" I said, "Yes, he works for a cardboard company and I'm trying to locate him. I'm sorry I troubled you." "This is strange," she said, "but he and his wife are in a social club with my husband and me."

She seemed so friendly that I shared my joy and surprise at having a wrong number turn out to be key in locating Jim. I explained why I wanted to talk to him and our conversation went on for nearly an hour.

I went to bed that night, planning on calling him first thing in the morning. I thanked God for the unusual course of events and fell asleep.

I was awakened at seven A.M. by the doorbell. *Who on earth could that be?* I grabbed my robe and made my way to the door. "Special Delivery letter for Rhea Zakich," a cheerful young man said. I signed for it and couldn't imagine who it could be from. I opened it and did not recognize the name. I slowly read,

> *Dear friend,*
>   *This is His money. I'd like for you to use it for the wonderful game you told me about on the telephone. If you can pay it back someday, fine. If not, that's all right. It belongs to God and He wants me to give it to you."*

Folded in the letter was a check for five hundred dollars. *"O God, how could I ever doubt that you would help me if I ask? Why do I stray from you when I know that?"*

With that money we paid for the printing and the other necessary things for the first batch of 100 games when they came off the press at Goodwill Industries. Those were sold before we finished gluing them to the cardboards. We ordered another 100 and with the help of a flyer announcing the game's availability, those were also sold.

Betts and I were beginning to tire of painting six different colored pegs for each game. There we were in our own game business, but it wasn't easy. I still didn't function too well in the business world.

My husband casually asked me one day if it had ever occurred to me that I should be paying sales tax for the games I'd sold. "Paying it?" I asked. "I'm not charging it." He suggested I go to the Board of Equalization and find out how to handle selling and sales tax. How ridiculous not to have thought of something like that, and I never would have known whom to contact to find out about it.

I *had* been charging for the games, at least the last hundred (the first hundred I gave away). But I hadn't kept any records and I had changed the price many times depending on whether I needed to buy paint or more cardboard.

So I made an appointment to talk to someone about how to handle my tax obligations. When I went, I couldn't answer the questions they asked. I didn't have a business license. I'd have to

106

apply for a business license and get a resale number. I would have to file several reports, pay certain fees, etc. It seemed overwhelming to someone who never handled the money in the household.

A few days later when I was up to my neck in paperwork, I got a phone call from Goodwill saying they could no longer do the game papers for me because they were taking on a new project. I found a professional printer who would print three hundred copies for me, so I placed the order and in three days picked up a stack of beautiful shiny papers to be mounted.

Someone told me about a new kind of glue that came in a spray can, which would certainly streamline the gluing process so I ordered a case. Not only had I spent the five hundred dollars given me, I had also now soaked up another five hundred dollars with the bills coming due the next month.

Then disaster struck.

I spent hours one evening trying to figure out forms for going into business, but I just became frustrated. Around midnight, I tabled the paperwork and decided to glue some game boards so I could go to bed with some feeling of accomplishment anyway. I laid fifty cardboard squares all over my kitchen and family room floors. What a great idea, I thought; I'll mass produce these by spraying all these boards and then I'll smooth the beautiful game papers in place and tomorrow I'll have a whole stack of games ready to go.

In the morning I walked into the kitchen to receive the biggest shock ever! The game boards had curled up like giant potato chips. They were ruined. I tried to flatten them but they cracked. The glue had been too wet or something. $250 lost! I was sick.

I looked at the sight and didn't know how to express what I was feeling. That batch of games represented the money that was to pay the debts I'd run up. Dan still wasn't working. I couldn't imagine how we would pay the bills when they came. *That does it! That's the last straw. I give up.* "God! *I don't understand you! Where do you go when I need you?*"

I cried as I stacked the curled boards up and stomped them in my trash barrel. A part of me died that day as I decided to go out of business.

Chapter 18

Rescued

Because I couldn't express my sadness to anyone, it came out of me as anger. I cleaned my kitchen and living room, removing all traces of the game business. I sprayed floral scented perfume around to cancel out the glue and paint smell my family had gotten used to. I was abrupt with everyone and everything as I tried to pretend that it didn't matter. Under my breath I was muttering, *"All right God, I quit! If you want this game out in the world, you do it! I was willing to help you, but there must be something I'm doing wrong or something I don't understand, so count me out!"*

My family was shocked when I announced that I went out of the game business, but they didn't complain. For the first time in months, they could walk through a room without having to step over stacks of uncollated cards, game boards with glue drying, freshly painted pegs, and stacks of empty boxes. And they could breathe more freely, too.

After a few days, there wasn't a mention of the game. I was so sure that God was going to be sorry he didn't help me that I could act as if I didn't care until he got in touch with me again.

Meanwhile, a young boy from our neighborhood noticed the crinkled game boards awaiting trash pickup and decided to help himself to one. Since I had thrown out all the other game items, he was able to get a complete set of everything necessary to play *Tell It Like It Is*. His mother, a nursing instructor, looked it over and decided that it would fit nicely in her nursing program. She saw it as a way to take students beyond medical terminology and sterile procedures and help them learn to relate to patients' feelings and perhaps to their coded messages.

She used the game with her nursing students with amazing results. The students seemed to become more sensitive to each other and to their patients after they engaged in it for a while. The instructor was excited about this crude, handmade game, so she asked her son where he had gotten it. He reported that it had been destined for the trash pickup down the street at the Zakiches.

I didn't know his mother, although I had seen her a few times in her front yard and usually gave a neighborly wave as I drove by. I had no way of knowing that she had recently joined with a young man in a partnership to produce medical teaching aids. Their company was one mile from my house. She showed my game to her partner, and the two of them saw great potential in it.

Needless to say, I was startled to receive a phone call from a stranger asking if I'd ever considered putting my game on the market. I thought one of my friends was pulling a prank. I tried to control myself and act cool. "Oh, I thought about it, but I don't really think I'll do any more with it."

He went on to say, "Seriously, I think this game has tremendous possibilities and I'd like to talk to you about marketing it." It began to penetrate that this man was serious. I consented to meet with Mr. Herndon, but I couldn't get over the fact that I'd written so many letters to companies all over the country, and here were two people less than two miles away asking me if they could produce and market my game.

As I drove to the office where Au-Vid Inc. was located, I felt suspicion seep into me. Friends had warned me about people who try to steal ideas and capitalize on them. What if he was trying to take advantage?

I arrived at the address, took a deep breath, and said a short prayer asking God to give me wisdom and to remove suspicion from me.

The moment I stepped inside that office, I knew I was in the right pace. It felt like home to my spirit. There was instant rapport between Mr. Herndon and me. I knew I could trust him. He told me how excited he was about the possibilities he saw in *Tell It*

Like It Is, and I in turn shared my briefcase full of letters from people who'd had a life-changing experience.

Excitement rose as we went through the letters one by one and marveled at all that had happened. One in particular spoke to him. A professional businessman wrote, "My teen-age daughter and I hadn't actually talked for about a year, but last night with your game we were able to really communicate. I love my daughter and was able to tell her for the first time in years. Thank you for creating such a wonderful tool. P.S. *Tell It Like It Is* should never be called a game because it's NOT a game! It's more of a non-game!" We continued to read more letters, and time and time again someone said "Don't call this beautiful experience a game."

Mr. Herndon gathered several of his staff together and all of us played for about an hour. By the end of the time, it hit us – it's not a game, it's an Ungame®! We all liked the sound of it, so my "baby" was christened with a new name. I felt as if I was putting my game in a foster home where it could be better cared for. We drew up a contract.

That night as I went to bed, I again marveled at how God seems to come through in my life. I shared my joy with him. *"Father, Father. Why do I ever doubt you? Why do I doubt myself? Help me to trust you more. Thank you for teaching me that once I let go, you would show me where the game belonged. O God, help me learn how to release and when to release."*

I spent a lot of time in the coming weeks thinking about releasing. Letting go and letting God. I had heard that phrase many times. Why was it so hard for me? It was revealed to me in a prayer time that my role in many things was to be that of starter, initiator, a creator. Many times it would be someone else's responsibility to take the project to the next step. I could see how I had complicated my life by thinking that just because God gave me an idea, he expected me to take it all the way to fruition.

In my three months of silence, I became disconnected from everything that I had been doing before. Prior to losing my voice, I had been involved in all sorts of busy-ness, but now, people were used to my being gone. For a couple years, all my energy was put into making handmade games. Now it was out of my hands.

I returned home and had a sobering thought that I needed a life. But, what did I want to do? Then it hit me that very few people have such a clean slate. I had a healthy body. I had all the things I had learned, and I could actually design my life. I felt truly blessed.

I decided I was going to venture out into the world, and I was going to design a life based on what I had learned in those three months of silence.

Chapter 19

Moving Forward

When I reflected on what I had learned in creating the game, what came to mind first were the people who came to my house in the early stages, often one at a time, sitting across from me and sharing things that they had never shared before. I realized they knew I wouldn't tell anybody because I was a mute. I wouldn't judge, I wouldn't interrogate, I wouldn't probe, I wouldn't laugh, or make jokes about their experience. This was such a revelation to me. I didn't know that other people were walking around with sadness or fears because they didn't talk about it.

The next stage of my life unfolded as a result of these experiences. I brought small groups of people into my home, sat them around my handmade game board and heard them talk about their feelings.

I started with a dozen women, meeting weekly for six weeks or so. This created an interesting momentum. Somebody would bring her sister-in-law from another city, then I'd get a call asking if I would come and lead something with women in their church or PTA group. I always said "yes." This became my new career. One invitation led to another. I didn't consciously seek any of them.

I heard the same kinds of stories over and over. "I've never shared that with anyone before." "You know, it's amazing. Mary usually dominates every session, but when you're there she's very quiet." And then they'd say, "And, Cynthia, who never talks seemed to open up and talk a lot."

The main thing I learned was that people felt safe in small groups. When people played the game and discovered no one could talk unless it was their turn, they somehow felt it was alright to risk saying something they had always kept inside.

I remember the story of Norman who shared something he'd never talked about before.

Dan and I had two couples over to play the Ungame® one evening. We had bowled and played cards with them so we figured we knew them pretty well, but found out this night there was a subject that had never come up before.

We'd played around the game board for about 45 minutes answering questions about favorite vacation spots, what we'd like for our next birthday, our definition of success, etc., until Norman, a rather quiet guy, drew this card, "Talk about a time when you felt guilty." He hesitated a long time before saying, "I always feel guilty." Since the Ungame® rules say no one can talk except on his turn, we sat in silence waiting for him to either continue or pass the dice to the next person. His expression changed and he looked down at the table. We waited.

"I guess it began when I was eleven years old. I've felt guilty ever since then." After what seemed like a long time, he began to tell a story. "Our uncle used to take me and my older brother, Ralphie, fishing every Saturday. But this one Saturday he wasn't able to take us, so we asked our mom to let us go alone. She decided, after much begging, to let us take our fishing poles and walk the mile of winding dirt road to the lake. There was no one there that morning, so we had the small dock to ourselves." Again, there was silence that, in any other circumstance would surely have been filled with questions or chatter. But we just sat there, ready to listen.

"Ralphie and I didn't always get along. He was older, had a lot of friends and liked school. I had trouble making friends and getting good grades, and I didn't like that Ralphie always got privileges before I did." We wondered where this story was going as we watched Norman's demeanor change. It was as though he was reliving some painful experience. I believe it was the first time

114

I felt someone's pain without knowing the reason. An eerie hush filled the room as five people waited to hear Norman's next sentence. He began to pour out the story of a skirmish with his brother that escalated to a wrestling match. Then with tears in his eyes, he said, "I knew Ralphie couldn't swim … but I pushed him off the dock. Oh God, I remember watching him flail, trying to find something to hold on to, but I couldn't help him. I thought, "I have to go tell mom and find someone to help him!"

I remember gripping the table, wanting so much to say something to comfort him, but, it was as though we were all suspended in some strange time zone, hovering over each word and experiencing Norman's emotions with him.

As though in a trance, Norman described running the mile home, telling his mom that Ralphie fell in the lake, and how she ran to a neighbor who had a truck. They went to another neighbor who had a small boat. Around the table we could all feel the terror of little Norman running behind the truck on the dusty, dirt road to the lake and the dock. But nothing compared to the pain we felt when he described hiding behind a rock, watching the men drag the lake and pull up Ralphie's lifeless body. Tears were flowing from all of our eyes, and Norman's wife's reaction made it clear that she'd never heard the story before.

Now there was a long pause. I don't think any of us had moved a muscle during the story. Norman kept the card in his hand, so we waited having no idea what more he might say.

Hearing him describe the funeral was equally gripping. We could imagine the little boy greeting people at the door and being pushed aside as they cried, "Oh, poor Ralphie."

"*I* was poor, but nobody knew," Norman said. Then he returned to the card in his hand and said, "I've never told anyone that I pushed him, and I've felt guilty every day of my life." He slid the dice over to the person to his left.

Oh my goodness, I thought. What are we supposed to do with THAT? Should we put the game away? Do we throw out the rules and talk about this? Should we pray?

Before I could settle my mind, Margaret rolled the dice, moved her marker and took a card. *Dear God, don't let it be a card about the animal you'd like to be or about your favorite restaurant!*

Her card said, "Say something about trust." She looked at Norman and said, "Thank you for trusting us with that story." We all nodded our concurrence. But the next player was able to wrap up the game by landing on the space that gives permission to make a comment on any subject. Bruce pushed his chair back from the table and mumbled, "This is going to be a non-verbal comment," as he got up and walked around the table, dropped to his knees and with tears, embraced Norman and said, "Come here, you big son-of-a-gun." We all cried now. The kind of cry that is releasing and cleansing. There were no words, just incredible love flowing. We knew then the game had served its purpose and we could put it back in the box until next time.

Weeks later Norman's wife told me how he had changed since that night. He was laughing more, relating better to their sons, and actually seemed to be standing taller. He'd been set free and was finally healed. I was sorry that he'd had to wait forty years to find a safe place to share such a heavy burden.

~

As I was going through my "learning process" I would share it in presentations with school psychologists, teachers, counselors, pastors, and the like. I was getting a reputation as begin a spicy and fun speaker who could make the audience laugh and cry in the same hour. I began to get a lot of bookings, and there was a time when I was booked two years in advance. I spoke three to five times a week to the Rotary Club, the Kiwanis, the PTA, and church groups.

Before long, I wanted more time. I felt that talking to groups for twenty minutes was fine, but it didn't really change anybody. So I designed some communication workshops and the extended time allowed the participants to experience the principles rather than just hear about them. Some of the workshops evolved into weekend retreats in the mountains. And the word continued to spread.

Some of the booklets I created for classes I led.

The sensitivity movement emerged around the same time the Ungame® came out, but I was unaware of it. I had never heard of encounter groups. When I heard people talk about feelings and going to Esalen Institute and the like, I said to myself, "I know what they're doing." But the amazing thing to me is that it came from somewhere inside, not from out there.

If we truly get in touch with the Holy Spirit, then we really don't need all the books, or games, or anything. If you understand why this works you don't need them. But until you get it, until you truly open your heart and discover what the Holy Spirit can do, books and the Ungame® and other tools will help you get there. We have access to so much wisdom, yet we rely so much on external sources that it doesn't become real. Until we discover it for ourselves, it's not ours.

The more I listened to people's stories and experiences, the more I realized that most of the problems were symptoms of deeper issues. Whatever they were mad about was not the real problem. I began to hear beneath the words. They'd talk about whatever was ailing them, and as I listened I could usually connect their words to the physical/emotional source.

Sometimes I'd tell audience members to take out a piece of paper and write down their biggest problem. Most people immediately wrote it down. Then I said, "Guess what, that's not your biggest problem. It's just a symptom. Ask yourself why you have that problem."

And they wrote down that answer. Maybe their biggest problem was they were broke, and I'd say, "What's that a symptom of?" They answered, "Well, I haven't been working for a long time." I said, "That's not your problem either. Why haven't you been working for a long time" "Because I don't go out and look for jobs." "That's not your biggest problem either. Why don't you get out and look for jobs?" "I've been depressed." "Why have you been depressed?" "Well, I don't feel good about myself. I don't feel I have anything to offer." "Now we're getting closer to the problem."

The process can go deeper and deeper, and what they thought was the problem was really a symptom of a larger issue. If the deepest problem can be unearthed, healing can begin.

One morning when I was hosting a women's prayer group, my next door neighbor, Gladys, came crying into the house. It was unusual to have someone boohooing in front of a group in those days, so we all stopped what we were doing and asked her what was wrong.

She sobbed, "I'm afraid John is going to leave me, I'm afraid we're going to get a divorce."

One of the women immediately said, "Let's pray that they get back together."

"Wait a minute, I want to hear more." I said. "Gladys, what's happening between you and John?"

"It's his rage. He got so angry that he ran his fist through the cupboard door the other day, and he hits the wall. I'm afraid he's going to kill me."

Somebody said, "We had better pray about John's rage."

118

"Wait a minute," I said. "I know John and he's a mild mannered guy. What sets him off?"

"Well, mostly when I've been drinking."

Silence.

Then someone said, "I didn't know you had a drinking problem. Come on, let's all pray that Gladys gets over her drinking problem."

I knew this wasn't the core of the problem either. "Gladys, we're together every day, when are you drinking?"

She answered, "Ever since John got that job. He's gone two or three weeks at a time. I just hate this job."

Someone said, "Well, let's all pray for John to get another job."

I still wasn't buying it. "What happens when John's gone a long time?"

"Well you know, the first week is okay, I keep busy. Then I start to get lonely. By the third week I get really depressed and I start drinking."

I knew the Holy Spirit was leading me.

"What does it feel like?"

"I'm afraid."

"Of what?"

"That John will find somebody else." Then she started to cry. "I'm afraid I'll be abandoned again like I was when I was a little girl." At this point, she began to scream, "**Abandoned like when I was a little girl!**"

I felt we had peeled back the layers to the source of the problem, so I suggested that we pray about it. She had never been healed of what happened when she was three years old when her daddy left and never came back home. Nobody every explained anything to her. She told us later how she would sit on the curb every day, watching for her daddy's car. She said she never played, she never really had a childhood. As an adult, this unresolved issue started to surface in her marriage through her anxieties and stress.

During the same time, because of my interest in this sort of work, I started to find people who knew much more about these things than I did. I found mentors and healers to study with and observe.

In many ways, my inside-out way of working was confirmed by the teachings of these healers. Indeed, the outer symptoms always had deeper roots. I started to lead healing workshops, which involved taking the person back to their original pain, opening it up, and allowing Jesus to heal the memory.

I also learned during that time to have a continual dialogue with God. Every thought I had, I'd share with God. It was like an ongoing conversation. I'd be with a person and at the same time ask God, *"Okay God, what do I say next? I don't know what I'm doing."* Then a thought would just come and I learned how to speak it. It was profound – and it worked. I began to trust that inner dialogue.

When I met with someone, whether in my living room or around the game table, and I suspected that what they'd been sharing were really symptoms, I would feel a deep sense of compassion. I wanted them to know that they were focusing all their energy in the wrong direction. So many of them were going through all those self-help programs, trying to stop smoking, or drinking, or to get their eating habits under control.

Occasionally, after time together I would walk with the person for a while and say, "I really feel your hurt when you talk about not having your mother. If you ever want to talk about it, I think I would like to hear it. Maybe I could help you deal with some of the pain around it. If you feel up to it, let me know."

A week, two months, maybe a year later I'd get a call. "Remember when you said you'd be willing to be there and help me through my pain?" And I'd say, "Sure, let's get together."

I discovered it was best to work with someone for a large chunk of time. When someone asked me to work with them, I never decided on the spot. I would take a day or so, ask God about how much time this person would take, and he would give me an answer. While doing counseling this way, I learned from experience that if we set aside nine hours (or twelve, or twenty), the breakthrough would happen somewhere in the final hours. This never ceased to amaze me, but it helped me trust the advice I was getting from God.

There were incredible transformations in the lives of these people. They were never the same. I'm still in touch with many of them; they never returned to their original states of pain.

Chapter 20

On Tour

By 1978, the Ungame® had been out for six years and had spread from Southern California (where we could market it) all across the country. So the Ungame® Company hired a firm to send me on public relations tours, and I traveled three months out of the year, September through Christmas time.

Rhea Zakich, an Orange County, California housewife with a high school education, became this sought-after television personality. It was an exciting time, it certainly stretched me out of my comfort zone.

I knew Regis Philbin before he became famous. He interviewed me in Los Angeles and in Pittsburg, two different locations where he had TV shows during those days. I would do an interview with a big newspaper and be on two or three television programs and a couple of radio shows in every city. In a way, it was kind of a glamorous life. It was also stressful, but people found that hard to believe. They'd hear that I was traveling to twenty-six cities every year, and it sounded exciting. But it was also very grueling. I learned how to do it – and do it well. Sales of the game went up in every city I toured.

On the Evening News in Chicago in 1991

The goal for a lot of interviewers is to tease the person they are interviewing. Sometimes I had the feeling that their entire purpose was to make a fool of me. They'd ask questions like, "What are you trying to do, make a million bucks out of this?" Or, "Who needs a game just to get people talking?"

They tried their little tricks, but I learned to come right back at them.

One woman was especially cruel on a radio interview. She started by saying, "Our next guest is a woman from California. She's invented a game and she obviously thinks this is the answer to the world's problems, but personally I played it last night with a group of friends and it was boring." And then she proceeds to say… "Please welcome our guest, Rhea Zakich."

It's not fun to say "hello" after an introduction like that, but my response was, "It tells me more about your friends than it does the game. You see, I played it yesterday too, and people laughed and told great stories. So I guess it's all about who you hang around with."

This totally disarmed her and I had complete control for the rest of the interview. Her tone changed immediately. "How did you get them all to be honest?"

I answered, "Well, it's tough sometimes. Some people can insist on being superficial, just joking or laughing, but if they begin to trust, they'll open up."

Another time a female interviewer asked, "What do you think of a husband who won't open up and share his feelings?" I just said, "I think he doesn't trust his wife."

There again, she didn't know where to go. I'd listen in the green room to other interviews and I would learn the style of the person before I went out there. This particular woman was going to bash men, no doubt about it, so I added, "I know what you mean, a lot of men have grown up in families where they got the impression they shouldn't have feelings or shouldn't share them. That makes it difficult." I was on her side after that.

I got good at comebacks, and interviewers had to keep going; a split second in television is very valuable. I just got better and better, but some people were really vicious. I recall one male interviewer saying, "I think this game is stupid. I don't care what other people think and I don't want them to know what I think."

I responded with, "I'd like to talk to your wife or to your best friend."

All in all, the interviews ended up being very good. Even the more contentious interviewers decided to like me afterwards. They wrote raving reviews and said the interviews were very spicy.

With Maureen Reagan on a Talk Show in 1990

Still, you always had to be on top of the interviews to answer questions like, "How much money do you get out of this?" "What are your royalties?" "How did you get the game on the market?"

Those kinds of questions and answers don't increase sales. To make sure the interviews went in the right direction, I gave them cards with typical questions that I could answer.

In some cases, I was told that the interview couldn't be a commercial, so we'd talk about family communication. If the game was going to be mentioned it had to be mentioned by them. This was all clarified back in the green room by the producer. I always agreed not to bring up the game. I played by their rules, but it was amazing how we could get a good plug in for the game. Many times, halfway through the interview, the interviewer would reach down to the coffee table and say, "Well, she's invented this game," and they held it up.

By 1990, we passed one million in sales, the game was translated into different languages, and it was becoming popular in far-away places like Australia, England, and France.

Doing PR was a wonderful experience, but it interrupted the healing kind of work I was doing with people. There I was, doing interviews – three minutes on the noon news in Minneapolis, or seven minutes on a morning talk show in Tampa. What can you say in such a short time? My job was to tell them about the communication game, but I had to talk fast. It was boosting game sales, but it wasn't changing lives the way I had learned lives could be changed.

After twelve years of this schedule, I finally opted to drop the PR tours. The company was concerned that the game sales were going to drop to almost zero, "Because the only way people will buy the product is with you being in their town." There was no Internet and no paid advertising from the game company.

I felt really bad about letting them down, but I had little choice. It was keeping me from my healing work. It just seemed like it was time for me to be done with it. I enjoyed it while I was doing it, I liked what it did for me, but in 1991 I officially moved into my other life. I preferred to lift a few people to a higher place than reach a million with one game commercial.

Many people in the healing field like psychologists, psychiatrists, and counselors wrote me letters and told how they used the game to make a bridge with their clients. I've had hundreds of letters over the years, and I share this one as an example.

Dear Rhea,

I work as a psychiatric technician in the psychiatric unit of a small community hospital. We serve people who are depressed, manic, suicidal, and homicidal and panic stricken. We help people who are struggling with everything from substance addiction to schizophrenia, including a myriad of psychiatric and personality disorders. Over the course of the past year, I have played the Ungame® with people suffering from all of the above. And I need to tell you that it has never let me down. I want to thank God and you so very much for creating this miracle. It provides a fantastic way to bring about communication and cohesion on the unit. And because I play along, it allows me to have much greater rapport with the patients. The groups become more of a "we" instead of an "us" and "them."

I could go on for pages about my wonderful experiences with the game... about the countless times I have been amazed to see people open up and talk about things that they've never talked about, that they've never thought about, or, sadly, have not had anyone to talk with about.

I remember one woman who was suffering from bipolar disorder and was extremely manic at the time. She felt a compulsion to speak almost constantly. She did agree to play the game but wanted to play by the rules, and she had to literally hold her hand over her mouth so as not to speak before her turn. She said that playing the Ungame® helped her to gain a feeling of control over her behavior, when she had been feeling very out of control. It also gave her a strong sense of accomplishment.

Then there was this man who was socially withdrawn - more deeply than I have ever seen someone withdraw. He made no eye contact, strictly spoke only when spoken to, and almost always answered in one word sentences. Over time, he began to show some slow improvement, and one day I convinced him to join in on a game. His peers were very gentle and patient with him, and he was able to become more comfortable with the situation. Over the course of the next few days, we played as much as we could. He opened up more and more and was eventually able to not only answer questions fully, but could generate thoughtful comments and questions for others.

These are only two examples of what I have seen transpire during what some would look at as just a simple game. Thanks again.

Sincerely,
David Bolen, BS
Psychiatric Technician

At the Christian Booksellers Convention approx. 1988

Yes, by then millions of people were being touched by the Ungame®. But almost from the beginning, I realized that *I was the one receiving the most benefit*. In the process of playing this game (and having to answer my own questions), I found out that I didn't really know myself. I didn't know what I believed. I didn't know what I thought. I didn't know what I felt. So there I was - creating questions that I wanted to ask other people, but in the game, I would have to answer them myself.

I answered at a level of truth when playing the game, but I continued thinking for days after, that there was something else beneath the answer, and something else beneath that. Being encouraged to answer the question began a layer-by-layer process of uncovering who I am. Through the years I had buried the "real me" under a pile of pretense.

Chapter 21

Teaching and Healing

So what was I to do with all I had learned and was learning? I knew that one of my spiritual gifts was teaching. However, I learned to ask what the agenda was for the group I was speaking to. One time I was asked to speak on healing on Friday and Saturday night at a women's retreat. I prayed and prepared two lessons, the first one being an introduction and the second one the application of what we'd talked about. We would offer a healing experience.

Well, what was I to do when the ladies showed up for the Saturday night session in Halloween costumes? Giggling and laughing. Needless, to say, my plan didn't work as well because I hadn't been informed about the party following my session.

I also learned to ask about the meeting room and how it was arranged. People will connect sooner if they are all on chairs of the same height, rather than a mixture of sofas, chairs, etc. It's important to sit in a circle close together because people are more apt to participate if they don't have to project their voices. When the group was large, I put chairs in a "U" shape with an aisle or two, so attendees could see the faces across from them.

I found it's the little things that are most important when leading a group. If I want to offer something that will change their lives, 80% of it depends on the atmosphere! The Holy Spirit will enter when the hearts are open. And after all, the Holy Spirit is the Teacher *(But when the Spirit of truth comes, he will guide you into all the truth. John 16:13)* So it is important to create the environment (tangible things) and the atmosphere (the intangibles) at the very beginning.

Success, for me, changed from wanting to accomplish 'my' plan, to wanting to change lives, which meant I needed God's help. I learned to be sensitive to the people in front of me as well as the

Holy Spirit who would speak to me in a still small voice. I became so sensitive that I could walk into a room of strangers and tell right away whether the people were connected or separate, open or closed. If I'd been invited to speak on a serious topic, and some of the women came just to have fun, I could feel the lack of harmony in the group. Of course that made it more challenging.

This taught me to help the planning committee craft their invitation to their group so the purpose was clear. For example, if the event is just to 'get away' for a vacation, make it clear. If it's for spiritual growth, or learning to pray, make that clear. Then they come with the same expectations and no one is disappointed. I could feel the unity in the groups when everyone came for the same reason. The Spirit in the room was very different when those who came were hungry for the topic (whether it was prayer, healing, or parables), and the group unified more quickly, which caused people to feel safe to be open and honest in their sharing. To me this was vital.

I'm reminded of a retreat I was invited to lead in Northern California (before I learned about setting forth the expectations). I was asked to speak on healing Friday evening, and all day Saturday. I was excited and prepared. However, the group seemed fragmented with some coming to the sessions late or getting up in the middle to get coffee.

I was heartsick when I showed up for the Saturday afternoon session to find that about a fourth of the ladies had left the retreat to go shopping. They hadn't understood what the committee wanted. Their brochure made it look like a "getaway" rather than a "go to." I tried to keep a hopeful attitude even though I was hurt that they didn't 'like' what I was doing. So, knowing I'd see them in the dining hall, I prayed after my session that I could be gracious and forgiving when they returned, and with God's help, I was able to let it go. It's almost impossible for me to hear from the Holy Spirit when I'm hurt or "ticked off."

Here's the interesting thing... I flew home feeling somewhat like a failure. Dan picked me up at the airport and drove me home where our little granddaughters were turning cartwheels in the front yard. Wanting to connect with them, I said, "Watch me, girls! I can do a cartwheel!" even though I hadn't tried one for thirty years. Well, I fell on my back on the root of our big tree and felt excruciating pain. I couldn't move and had to be carried into the house. Dan took me to the hospital where the x-rays showed I had two crushed vertebrae and was told they wouldn't know for a few days if I'd be able to use my legs. I was strapped on an examining table with my neck and head in a brace and straps everywhere to keep me from moving. Eventually, Dan went home and I felt deep despair, as well as pain.

During the night, I heard the Holy Spirit say, *"Ask those women to pray for your healing."* My first thought was, "A lot of them walked out and didn't even hear half of my teaching!" The thought kept coming, and my feelings showed me that I hadn't really forgiven them. I didn't want them to know that now *I* needed healing.

When Dan came to see me I asked him to look on my desk, find the leader's phone number, and tell her to ask all the ladies to pray for my healing. He said he would, and then he left to go to work. I still had not moved a muscle and the pain was such that I was afraid to even try. I knew there were straps holding me still but I couldn't see them because of my neck and head brace. I had no concept of time and couldn't see a clock (not that it would have mattered).

I dozed off. When I woke up I felt a strange sensation near my feet, but of course I couldn't look down. It was like a warm blanket being slowly pulled up. As the feeling continued up my body, I noticed that there was no pain in the parts that were being covered. I imagined that a doctor or nurse was covering me, but I couldn't see anyone. When it got up to my neck I became aware that all pain was *gone*. It was a day later when I was unrestricted that we all realized I was healed and could move freely.

I found out three days later, when I received a card signed by the whole group of women, that they had *all* prayed for me. That was thirty years ago, and I've never had any pain or problem with my back since. Surely a miracle! It taught me never to judge something as a failure when God is involved. What do I know?

In weekend retreats or workshops I led, we would start by playing the Ungame® on Friday evening to get to know each other. Midway through Saturday, I'd select one or two people in the group who seemed to be in serious crisis. By Saturday evening, I'd ask them if they were willing to let us go with them to the root of their pain and deal with it.

Leading one of my workshops.

When I minister to an individual, I try to get underneath the symptoms and down to the problem. I open with a prayer and then use a form of guided meditation wherein they close their eyes and we call on God, Jesus, the Holy Spirit – whatever words they're familiar with. We ask God to take them back to the root of the problem. I can skip hours of counseling by praying like this. For example, if I'm working with a woman who has a fear, I simply say, "Lord, you know where this all began, this fear of being in front of people that has affected her jobs both past and present. Please take her back there."

Then we sit in silence and let the process unfold. She might say, "I see a tree."

"Can you tell us about the tree? What does it look like?"

"It's a big tree."

"Where is the tree?"

(I'm not asking these questions like a quiz. I enter into what she is seeing and softy invite her to continue. There can be long periods of silence.)

"Well, it's in my Grandpa's backyard."

"How old are you when you're seeing this tree?"

"Three." And she starts to cry.

Out comes an experience that happened to her, that has been triggered. This experience wasn't about the symptoms, it was the cause of the problem.

When we go back to where she sees herself at three years old – under the tree where the drama happened, I ask her if she can believe Jesus was present. "See if you can see him."

This can be very difficult for some people. Sometimes people see Jesus in human form, other times as light, or they might just sense His presence. At that point, we ask Jesus to minister to the child in whatever way Jesus would do it. The form is not up to us. The woman describes what is happening. "He's coming to me, he's picking me up, he's holding me..." Then healing begins.

Chapter 22

Life Lessons Learned

Much of my training for my healing ministry came from the nearly one hundred Camps Farthest Out (CFO) family camps I attended over the years. The purpose of the week-long camps was to go 'farther out with Jesus' by experiencing and practicing living in the kingdom of God. There were camps in almost every state with 100-200 people of all ages who gave up TV, newspapers, and telephones for the week. It was a place where everyone let go of denominations and titles and was willing to follow a Spirit-led program that would train them to be "athletes of the Spirit." Believers came from many different places with the same goal of growing stronger in the things that matter—our personal relationship with Jesus Christ, to experience and practice Kingdom Living, and to take these skills back into our everyday life.

The CFO program of spiritual disciplines was developed by Glenn Clark, a college professor and athletic coach in 1930. Clark trained his athletes to become winning teams by teaching them to be disciplined and focused. He was also the teacher of an adult Bible class in a Congregational church. He wondered what would happen if he started training his class with the same discipline he trained his athletes. God gave him a dream to find a place where time and interruptions would not interfere with thoughts of the Kingdom. He prayed for a way to create something where people would not only talk about love and faith and a life of prayer, but would learn how to put these Christian virtues into practice.

The CFO schedule is designed with the belief that just as we breathe in and breathe out each day, our relationship with God should also be a time of taking in and giving out. Therefore, each CFO day includes times of taking in (listening to talks and listening for God to speak in times of meditation) and opportunities for outward expression (singing, writing, art, drama, and movement). From prayer groups (called Prayer Laboratories) to free time, each day offers the chance and the freedom to stretch and exercise your faith in new and refreshing ways. The camps were places where attendees could *taste* and *see* that God is good.

It was in these week-long retreats that I discovered much about God and prayer. I learned from hearing the stories of other campers and how God had worked in their lives. I got to sit at the feet of spiritual giants who lived and loved like Jesus. I witnessed miracles and indeed experienced them. I learned to pray in so many ways, and saw prayers answered before my eyes. Probably the greatest gift I received was being filled with the Holy Spirit and learning to hear God's voice when I pray. My prayers became dialogues rather than monologues. Listening to God became more important than going through my wish list asking God to do what I wanted. Thank you, God for CFO.

I attended camps for twenty years as a camper before becoming a speaker. That took me to many parts of North America and Australia. I continued attending two or three camps a year as a speaker for the next twenty years. During those years I came to see that people are all so different and each one needed a different kind of prayer. The Spirit would always surprise me with something I wouldn't have thought of. I began carrying a small suitcase with supplies I could use to help someone get in touch with their hidden hurt. I had art supplies, clay, pictures from magazines, a tape player and audio tapes of music (this was before CD's). So I was prepared to work with people in settings where meditating was not possible because of distractions or interruptions.

Chapter 23

Stories of Healing

I would like to share several stories of people who were healed during some of my retreats and workshops. (Names have been changed to protect the privacy of the individuals involved.)

One of my earliest healing experiences occurred in 1980. Andrew attended a six-week healing series and stayed after the last session. He had made no impression on me as he had never spoken in the class. When he began to talk, I remember breaking into a sweat. He had the worst stammer of any person I'd ever heard. I didn't know what to do with people like that. I just remember standing there at ten o'clock at night and being asked by this man in a business suit if I thought inner healing could help him. I said, "I believe something could be done."

Andrew said, "Will you-you-you pa-pa-pray for muh-muh-me right now?"

It had been a large class of nearly one hundred people. They were all streaming out the door so I asked my friend, Sheryl, if she'd stay behind. When everyone else was gone, we closed the door and I told Sheryl I'd like her to pray with me for this man. "His name is Andrew. He has difficulty speaking." (Sheryl had traveled with me to many retreats and was becoming a very gifted and sensitive prayer partner.)

We sat on the floor with Andrew between us. We found out he was fifty-four years old and he'd never had a real job. He was afraid to go to an interview, because of his stuttering problem. He finished furniture in his garage because he could do that with minimum interaction.

I told him that I didn't know what to pray for right then or what to do, so if he had the time we'd just be silent and see what came to me.

We sat there…

By this time in my life, I was aware of the many ways God spoke to me. One of the most frequent ways I get messages is through images. In the early part of my healing work, I thought my mind was wandering and I ignored these images, but eventually I learned to trust them.

As we're sitting there, I'm asking God what I should do with this man. Suddenly, I see an old-fashioned water pump. I hadn't seen a water pump like this since I was five and visiting my grandfather. My first reaction to this image was, "Man I'm tired, I've got to focus on this person."

Again, I pray silently asking God to help me. I see the same water pump, but I don't have the courage to say it. Sheryl (whose ways of hearing from God most often come in words) says, "I'm getting the word 'water,' does that mean anything to you Andrew?"

There is no response from Andrew, but I think *water… water…* "Well, I'm seeing an old water pump." I say.

Silence.

Over the years, I've learned that silence is no reason to panic, but in that moment I was a little nervous. And then I say, "Andrew, does that mean anything to you?"

Suddenly, he remembers living on a farm where they had a water pump and he is sad and starts to cry. He doubles over, holding his knees, sobbing. I say, "Andrew, you have to tell us what you are seeing."

He tells us (with no stammering whatsoever) that he's an only child, two-years-old, living on a farm. His mama is bathing him outside on a beautiful sunny day in a big wooden tub – using a water pump.

I say, "That sounds like a beautiful scene to me."

Andrew says, "She's singing a lullaby." Andrew sings it to us.

"Andrew, this sounds like a peaceful scene. Did something happen?"

All of a sudden, we feel him tense his body. "The fire, the fire!"

"Tell us about the fire."

Andrew continues to tell us that the barn is on fire. He sees his father, their horse and other barnyard animals running. They are on fire. His father is in flames.

"What is your mother doing?"

"She's running to be with Daddy, she needs to help Daddy!"

I ask what the little boy is doing.

"I'm screaming and screaming and screaming and screaming… He says it at least twenty times.

But while he's saying it, something registers in me - speech impediment. A child of two screamed and screamed for help and nobody came. Couldn't that affect his ability to speak? Couldn't that shadow his entire life?

He continues to describe how people came with buckets of water and put out the fire. He told me later that his dad lived. I don't know how long it was before someone discovered this little baby way over there in the field. He even described how the water coming out of the pump had scared him and that nobody was there. It was terrifying to this little baby.

When this drama unfolded down there on the floor, we were electrified hearing it. After Andrew took a couple of deep breaths, all three of us just rolled back against the sofa and lay there for a minute. I had to gather my wits and silently ask God what to do.

Then I knew. I told Andrew we had to go back to that little boy. I said, "We're going to rewind this film, Andrew, and I want you to go back and be the little boy, being bathed by your mother, and I want to hear that lullaby again."

That was scary for him, but he was willing. He had to work a little bit to get back there so I talked him through it. "Tell me about the tub, tell me about the pump." I asked if he could see the daisies growing. He could see that. "Tell me about your mom." Finally, he could hear the song.

It took some doing, but when we finally got back to the time just before the fire, I reminded him that Jesus was present. I asked him if he could see him.

There was a long, long wait. Then he kept saying, "No, no, I can't see him."

Then it hit me, he was focused on the barn and on his mother. So I said, "Andrew, turn around."

Suddenly, he said, "Oh yes, I see him. There he is."

Of course this is a joyous moment for me because it feels like I'm trying to walk on water here. Andrew sees him. This little baby sees the figure of Christ. Then we get to the fire part of the story, and I say, "Let's ask Jesus to protect this child." I don't try to lead Andrew in the situation. I don't tell him what Jesus does. It works best to have the individual tell me.

Andrew says Jesus picks him up.

"How does that feel?"

"He's holding me so tight. He's wrapping his robe around me and he's drying me off with his sleeves."

I certainly wouldn't have thought of that. I don't say anything, we just hold the image of this naked baby being held for a while. Then Andrew says, "Oh, I feel his heart beating next to my chest, my heart is beating the same as his heart."

I knew right then that something was happening in him that would change him. We savored this moment for a while, then we came out of it together and just looked at each other. Andrew stood up and stretched.

"I think this calls for a celebration. How can we do that?" I said. I still didn't know what effect this would have on his stuttering.

Without a hint of a stammer, Andrew suggested that we go to the ocean. "I'll tell you why. I've always been afraid of the water ever since I can remember. My wife always wanted me to go to the ocean with her, but I would never go. I want to go to the ocean."

We are eight miles from the beach and it is 11:30 at night. The three of us jump in Andrew's van and speed off. I think he

142

probably broke every speed limit. We get to State Park, drive right out in the sand, and jump out. Sheryl and I and this guy in a business suit run like crazy people through the sand and out into the ocean up to our waist. Andrew's throwing water up in the air yelling, "I can talk! I can talk!"

It was an incredible miracle.

I found out later that Andrew had a very traumatic experience at this exact spot on the beach. In second grade, his whole class went to Huntington Beach on a field trip. They were all supposed to go down to the water and look for seashells, but Andrew was afraid of the water so he tried to escape. He panicked. When the kids saw he was afraid of the water, they grabbed him and threw him into the ocean. The waves kept washing him up and the sand got into his nose and he sputtered and choked and couldn't speak. The kids teased him because he couldn't talk or play like the rest of them.

This story about Andrew is an example of the kind of thing I did for many years. Getting to the root and healing the original pain changes everything. The original pain sets us up for some additional dramatic things that can happen. For someone else, being thrown into the water at the age of seven may not have been so traumatic. But for Andrew, it unconsciously triggered the memory of being left in the tub with the water rushing in and nobody there to help him.

Andrew lost his speech impediment and began to speak clearly. He became active in a community theatre group in Los Angeles, and he sent me programs from the plays he was in. Later, he got a job with IBM. He had attended college before, but he had been too inhibited by his stammering to do anything with his degree.

~

Helen came with her husband to one of my classes on inner healing. On the first night, she came up to me and said, I'm here with my husband because he wanted to come." Helen had back trouble and she walked all bent over. She added, "If I have to get up and walk around it's because I can't sit very long." Here she was at almost a ninety-degree angle, carrying a pillow with her so she could sit, telling me she came to class because her husband wanted to come. I thought that was very interesting.

About the fourth session, I asked for a volunteer to be the subject of our prayer. We had talked for four, two-hour sessions about inner healing prayer, about how to pray for something that is hidden and deep within us that doesn't show like a broken leg does. Helen raised her hand, which was surprising because she was always acting like she was there for her husband.

She came up and sat on the chair, and the thirty-five of us in the class surround her with our chairs. I have her close her eyes, and I say, "Now Helen, we are going to pray that God will take you back in time to an incident or situation that needs a healing touch. I want you to just leave your mind wide open and be willing to report whatever comes into it. We're going to trust anything that shows up."

So I say a prayer and we sit in silence. After a time, I ask her if she is seeing anything, and she says she does. She starts to describe a scene that happened when she was five years old. She was an only child, and she sees herself on a farm with her dad. She likes to pal around with her daddy, she loves him and really enjoys working on the farm with him. They are buddies – she is closer to her dad than her mom.

Helen says, "I am five years old, I am with my daddy out in the front yard and a neighbor, Mr. Brown, comes across the road. I am listening to my daddy talk to Mr. Brown and my daddy says something and I say, 'Daddy, Daddy, that isn't what you told Mommy. You told Mommy _____.'" Then my daddy turns around and looks at me with fire in his eyes."

At this point, Helen is talking just like a five year old. She is deep in meditation. Her daddy is incredibly mad, squeezing her arm. He marches her back to the bedroom and says, "You stay here until I can deal with you." Then he leaves, slamming the door. She remembers sitting there not knowing what she had done. She had just told the truth, and her daddy had this terrible reaction. This

144

was a very unusual thing for her dad who had always been her buddy.

I asked her if she could tell us what happened when her daddy came back for her. She said "Yes" and proceeded with her experience. "My daddy comes in and he grabs my arm and marches me in the living room and then he takes a hot poker from the fireplace and pulls my pants down and hits my bottom with the poker. He tells me not to ever, ever, ever do that again. It is burning, burning my skin – ooh, my skin is coming off."

Helen was in pain there in the middle of this circle as she relived being hit with a red hot poker. I asked what happened next. She remembers going to school the next day. Her mother puts a long dress on her because she has welts all over her backside. She goes to kindergarten, which she loves. The teacher tells everybody to sit down but Helen can't sit down because of her bottom. The teacher keeps saying, "Helen, sit down honey, you're supposed to sit down." But Helen can't, so finally the teacher comes over and just plops her down in the chair. Helen tells us how much that hurt!

Since this was the hurt that needed healing, we had to back up the video. I said, "Helen, take a few deep breaths, let that picture fade and remember we are right here with you."

After Helen had a little break, I said, "All right, I want you to go back now to where you are standing in the yard with your dad and everything is fine." She could do this. She relived the incident up to the point where her dad had taken her into the living room by the fireplace. This is the part that needed healing so we prayed that Jesus would come into that scene and somehow handle this so that it would not leave a life-long scar.

Helen says that her dad has taken the poker out of the fireplace and he's pulled her pants down. She says, "He's going to hit me, he's going to hit me!" I feel beads of sweat dropping from my forehead. Suddenly, her demeanor shifts. I ask her what is happening. Helen says that Jesus has stepped between them and taken the blows. Helen feels so peaceful now. She is sitting calmly after this tremendous tension and saying, "Jesus is taking the blows with the poker."

I thought Jesus would comfort the little child because that is what he so often does in these meditations. Surprisingly, when I ask, "What is Jesus doing now?" she answers, "He is embracing my father and my father is crying." I wouldn't have thought that Jesus would comfort the man before he went to the little girl, but I have learned there are always surprises. And when the little girl saw Jesus hugging her father, she hugged his legs because she knew her daddy was not usually this mean.

When Helen came out of meditation, we were able to talk about this and how it affected her life for fifty years. The tell-tale signs were everywhere. Here is this woman who came in bent over. She had back trouble since she was a little girl. She had to bring a pillow to sit on.

I said, "Helen, I don't know you but have you been a person that never stood up for yourself because you were punished for being honest?" And she said, "Oh yes, I always feel like the victim, I've never had the courage to speak up all through my life." Of course she wouldn't because as a child she was punished viciously for telling the truth.

In addition, she couldn't sit down and she had all this back pain. So during the class in the following week, we had her lie down and we laid hands on her. We prayed that the pain that had taken up residence in the cells of her body from that trauma would be cleansed and flushed. I don't remember what words we used - often I invite other people to pray in their special way.

After her healing, Helen played tennis and rode a bike and was perfectly healthy after living with back pain for fifty years. This was one of my first occasions where I could see so clearly that our physical body carries the wounds.

~

In a deep meditation with Brenda, we went back to a time when she was nine years old, eating dinner with her mother, her pastor father and several brothers and sisters. They were all very active in their church. Brenda described sitting at the table not being able to eat and being scolded for it.

I asked Brenda why she wasn't eating. She said, "Because I know what is going to happen."

"What is going to happen?"

"My mother goes to meetings every night of the week."

I asked her if she was afraid to be away from her mother.

"No," she said, "but Daddy does bad things to me every night that mommy's gone to church meetings."

This little child was unable to eat night after night. She would be forced to eat or she would be sent to her bedroom for not eating. Then her mommy would go to her meeting which was a perfect opportunity for Daddy to come in the bedroom.

In this meditation, she told me about the night that she was so upset when her mommy left that she bolted from the table and hid in a guest room, which was off limits to the children. She described the terror of being under this big feather bed way back in the corner. She crouched back there listening to her dad's footsteps go all through the house looking for her.

We are hanging on her every word as she says, "He's getting closer, I hear him coming – he's coming – he's opening the door." Then she's quiet for a minute so I ask her what is happening. She says, "I see his shoes." She proceeds to describe this horrid scene to us from under the bed. She sees his feet and she knows he's going to get her. Then she tells how he reaches under the bed, grabbing for her until he gets hold of her arm and pulls her out.

Then she comes out of her meditation.

Brenda had asked for prayer for her relationship with her husband of fourteen years because she couldn't stand to be touched. She said, "Jack comes home from work sometimes during the day because he's in real estate. I never know when he'll show up. He'll walk in the house when I'm doing dishes, come up behind me and touch me. Once I turned around and hit him with the skillet. I yelled, "Don't you do that to me!" He never knows what he has done wrong. "One time I was cutting roses in the backyard in the middle of the afternoon. He had just finished his real estate work and he came over and he just touched me on the back. I took the bunch of rose stems grasped in my hand and slapped him with them. Then I felt horrible."

This is what she wanted prayer for. She had this anger that she didn't understand. Why would she attack her husband when he was just being loving? The connection between that and the poor, little nine-year-old hiding from her sexually abusive father was quite obvious to those of us in the prayer group. Every cell in your body will remember this kind of thing, so we knew it needed to be healed.

I assured her that Jesus was present somewhere. When people ask why he would let this happen in the first place, the only answer I know to give is based in scripture; Jesus is involved when someone asks him to be. He didn't heal everyone he saw – he healed the ones who came and asked for it or who were brought to him. He must have stepped over bodies in the same town. He knew the beggars, He knew the blind, but he only ministered to those who asked him.

I took Brenda back in meditation to the place where she was hiding from her father under the bed. I assured her that Jesus was there and that if she called on him, he would heal the situation. Brenda becomes still. She sees her dad's shoes from under the bed. I ask her if she could see Jesus. She says, "No, but I can see his sandals." (Of course, I would have never thought of this because I was viewing it from up above.) Brenda sees the sandals next to her father's shoes. Jesus would handle it from here. Indeed, she crawled out from under the bed, and Jesus took her in his arms. (I am always amazed how inviting Jesus into the picture changes it.)

Then Jesus lifted her father up from his knees and forgave him for what he'd been doing. This was the most powerful part of the experience. He not only rescued Brenda, he forgave the perpetrator, and consequently, Brenda was also able to forgive him.

There is nothing quite as powerful as the power of forgiveness. If we don't forgive what people have done to us and what we have done to others, like Brenda, we carry this baggage throughout our entire lives.

I noticed when Jenny walked into one of my classes, she had a person one either side of her holding her arms. Two neighbor ladies brought her, and it certainly seemed that she would not be able to manage without them.

I didn't know it at the time, but Jenny had agoraphobia – she was deathly afraid to leave her home. She lived two miles from the church where we were having class, but she hadn't been even a mile from her house in a decade. Somehow her two neighbors were able to bring her to this class for inner healing.

She came every week, but I didn't get to know her since the group had a hundred people. On the last day, the girls brought her up to me and said, "Jenny has not been out of her house for ten years and when we take her back home she will lock the door, terrified to come out." They asked if I would be willing to spend time with her – and I agreed to meet her at her home.

Once there, I asked her some questions to break the ice and get to know her. It was important to get her to relax and to build trust. Once we were comfortable together, we went into meditation.

I asked Jenny to be open and then asked the Holy Spirit to take her to a time in her life when all this began. She saw herself on a mountain road in the car with her mom and dad. They were driving in the Big Bear area where she grew up. She and her sister were teasing and joking and playing in the back seat and her mom kept telling them to settle down. "Quit poking each other and messing around." But they didn't.

At some point her father reached back in the car and tried to separate them and the car swerved and left the highway, rolling over and over. She and her sister survived. Her dad had some problems as a result of the accident, but he lived.

Her mother lived the rest of her life – paralyzed.

Jenny carried this tremendous guilt and never talked to anybody about it because nobody knew the reason they went off the cliff. In her mind, it was because she didn't quit tickling her sister.

I found out later that Jenny didn't avoid leaving her home until she reached a certain age – the age her mother was when they went off the cliff. She was afraid God would punish her - she would get killed or something bad would happen, so she decided if she never got in a car again, then maybe she wouldn't die. She was living with this secret fear.

So we prayed about it, but she couldn't see Jesus with her. She couldn't get there, so I said, "I'm having a retreat up in Big Bear next week and I think you need to go." She began trembling like a leaf so I asked her if I could talk to her husband about it. I told her I would drive us.

She said she would think about it. I called her every day of the week. Her husband wanted her to go. He told me he had her bed roll packed and everything was ready. When the day came, we literally led her to the car. She was walking stiff legged – she wanted to go but her body was all but paralyzed. But we managed to get her in the car.

I didn't realize at the time that I was risking my own life by driving Jenny to the retreat. Even before we got to the mountain road, while driving on the freeway, she was in great distress – all curled up on the seat next to me, babbling like a little baby. When we started up the mountain road, she reached over and started squeezing my arm so tightly that it was all I could do to make the turns. I couldn't tell her to let go because I feared she would open the door and jump out. (I had fingernail marks and bruises galore and my arm was sore for three weeks.)

Somehow or other, we arrived safely at Big Bear, and I got her up the last few steps and into the cabin. She immediately curled up in a little ball on the sofa. Soon other people began to arrive (some of who were from the other class Jenny had been in) so we did everything we could to keep her there for the whole weekend.

Her healing eventually happened in the process of taking her out for walks in the woods, praying with her, and counseling her. At the end of the retreat I wanted to say we "delivered" her home.

Jenny began getting out into the neighborhood and for the first time she saw the school her children attended. She went to the grocery store for the first time in years, and she began to take walks and do things with friends.

A few weeks later I got a call from Jenny saying her husband was on his way over to my house. He wanted to kill me because he said I ruined their marriage. Then she said, "He has a gun."

I remember plopping down in my chair thinking, *"Oh my God! What will I do? Do I jump in my car and get out of here? Do I lock the doors and not answer? I don't have a gun - I can't fight that way."*

As I sat there and waited, I calmed down a bit. I decided to stay put and see what happened. I leaned back and asked God what to do. I closed my eyes and saw an image of a mountain stream my husband and I used to go to in the Bishop area up in the Sierras. There was a beautiful babbling stream and I remembered our boys out there digging with sticks and turning rocks over. They would disturb the sediment and the water got murky. We told them they could drink the water when the dirt settled, but not when they were playing in it.

The meaning came to me instantly. I was scared because a rock had gotten turned over and all the dirt was coming up. If I could stay calm and trust that the Spirit could flow through me – like clear water – then I would have whatever I needed for this occasion. I took deep breaths and suddenly felt a sense of peace come over me. I heard the familiar scripture, "Be still and know that I am God," and I wasn't afraid any longer.

Ding dong! The doorbell rings. I take a deep breath and walk over to the door. I open it and look straight into Harold's eyes and just feel this tremendous compassion. I see the fear of a child. I see a little boy about to lose everything he's got. I look at him and say, "Oh, Harold." I push the screen door open and he walks in. I put my arms around him and he just melts. He hangs on me. He says, "I don't know what I am going to do. I don't know what I'm going to do. I think I'm going to lose Jenny."

He sits down on the couch. I sit on the floor with my hands on his knees and listen to him talk about how he thinks his marriage is on the rocks. I cry with him. I really don't say much to him but there comes a time when he is finished. "Well, thanks for listening." And he leaves.

Apparently things worked out for Harold and Jenny because years later I received a Christmas card from them. Jenny seemed radiantly happy and was involved in community activities. What a blessing to get feedback years later and to be able to see how this kind of healing can be such a turning point in one's life. I'm in the awe of the power of God.

~

Stan was fifty-six. He was a neat guy. He had worked as a landscaper for thirty years. We decided one day that we wanted to talk a bit longer so I suggested that we meet for lunch. He said, "I don't go into restaurants." That seemed a bit strange to me, but I suggested a park instead and Stan agreed.

During our meeting, I asked Stan why he didn't go into restaurants. He said, "I feel closed in. I'm afraid they will close the door." When I asked him what that was all about, his answer surprised me. He said, "I don't know. I have never been on a plane. I can't get on a train. If I drive in the car I have to have all the windows down. I can't get on elevators."

Stan had a pretty serious case of claustrophobia. He was a landscaper because most of his work was outside. He said he had learned to live his life to accommodate this problem. He said that his wife was one of the few people who knew about it.

He was ready to get to the bottom of it, so we prayed. When I asked the Holy Spirit to take Stan to back to when this all began, he went back...back...back and it was totally dark. He didn't know where he was or who he was – it was just dark. By things he was saying or the way he was describing it, I thought maybe he was in a closet, but he answered, "No, it is soft." Then I got a different image. I asked, "Are you in your mother's womb?" And he said, "I think so."

This was my first experience with taking somebody this far back. So now we were in the womb. At that point I'd known Stan for five years, but I didn't know he had a twin. I didn't think to ask if there was anybody in there with him, but he said it was crowded because of the other baby. And I said, "Were you a twin?" And he answered, "Yes."

Stan was born in the mid 1930's. In those days, if you lived on a farm there was a doctor who came with a bag - probably on horseback – to deliver the baby. Stan described being in the bedroom on this farm. There is a midwife there; the doctor has been called, but he hasn't arrived yet. His mother is in labor and the midwife is getting everything prepared and out comes a little crying baby. So the midwife takes the baby to the kitchen but Stan's aunt says, "She is bleeding, she is bleeding." The midwife tells her to tie the mother's legs together to stop the bleeding. They didn't know there was another baby in there.

So they tie the legs together until the doctor comes. Here is little baby Stan, ready to be born but he can't get out. As he describes it, it feels to him like he is going to drown. Nobody knows he is there. It is terrible! You wouldn't think a fetus could feel all this but he is describing it as if it's happening now.

Then the doctor comes, unties the legs and says, "Oh no, there is another baby here." Stan's father, who is watching all this take place, says, "Jesus Christ, not another one!"

This sets Stan up for life. Not only does he have serious fear of closed places, but he has to battle low self-esteem all his life.

Talking together after the meditation, I told Stan that I never knew he had a twin. He said, "Well, Sandra and I have never gotten along. She is very outgoing, and was popular and well known in school. She went on to become quite a professional business person. I was so shy, I never spoke up, I never talked in school, I didn't do well, I just stuck to myself. I felt useless."

I had Stan share this in the group the next week and somebody said, "Well Stan, how do you know you weren't just making it up that your dad said, 'Jesus Christ, not another one?'

153

How do you know he really said that?" Stan wasn't sure. Somebody else asked if there was anyone else alive who was there at his birth. Stan said he had a ninety-eight-year-old aunt living in Indiana, so he called her and asked her if she remembered his birth. She said, "Oh Honey, we didn't know there were two babies, and we thought your mother was bleeding to death so we tied her legs together." Then Stan asked her if she remembered anything anyone said at the time. She said, "Well, your father was so angry that he swore because he was going to have enough trouble paying for one baby."

Stan cried as he shared this with the group. "I always felt worthless. I've always felt like I was taking up space on the planet. I always thought I didn't have the right to even breathe the air because I wasn't supposed to be here." We were all crying with him.

Stan was healed and was fine after that. Amazingly, he went on to counsel prisoners. Before, he was deathly afraid of internal spaces, but he was able to go through gates and clanging doors that were locked behind him. He went down long corridors into the bowels of the prison to work with the inmates.

One of the reasons I share these stores is because they often trigger healings in the listeners – or readers – who have had similar experiences. I shared Stan's story at a retreat and received a letter from one of the attendees, a pastor who had a pre-birth experience of his own.

He wrote, *"I wanted to take a moment to thank you for the wonderful gift you gave us a couple of weeks ago at our retreat. We are still talking about our various experiences. I have been led to learn all about the healing of memories so I can incorporate this into my ministry. Personally, I have become aware of a pattern of behavior emanating from my pre-birth experience. Fifteen years of AA meetings and traditional therapy never quite touched the issue as that one memory did."*

I never learned what this pastor's story was, but I've come to understand that pre-birth can often be traumatic for both the babies and their parents. Some parents get angry because they are not ready for children yet, or they are fearful that they won't be perfect. Unfortunately, the child picks this up and remembers it for a lifetime

Chapter 24

Changed

I learned so much about myself and others on the course of this uphill-and-downhill journey. As I spoke to many groups around the country and even overseas, I shared my insights with my audiences.

When we are finally quiet and actually listen to a person, we start to get in touch with the feelings of the person talking. I've come to find out I'm a good listener. I've conditioned myself. I used to be a saver, a solver, a fixer. Now I can listen.

I've not only learned to listen, I've learned to listen beyond words. I often wrote songs to go along with my workshop and retreat topics, and I invited the audiences to sing along with me as I played my guitar. The chorus to one of the songs (entitled *Words Get in the Way*) went like this. "*I came to give my love to you, to brighten up your day. I want to listen to your heart but words get in the way.*"

I feel that in the process, I've learned quite a lot about people, and that's helped me to understand and accept, to empathize and be less critical of others. Maybe the most amazing part of all this is what I learned about my old friends and acquaintances. I'd be sitting across from people that I thought I really knew. They'd say the same things all the time, the same jokes, always the same sarcasm. Suddenly, it would hit me like a ton of bricks, "They are so lonely."

Instead of getting irritated at them for recirculating the same old answers, I was hearing at a different level. I began to hear beyond the words. In fact, the words that came out of people's mouths sometimes didn't even register. I watched how they folded the card or sweated or stuttered. I had never paid attention to that before because my brain was always popping with my ideas and thoughts which I felt no one had ever heard.

Maybe someone talked about anger and shared something their father did to make them furious. I'd hear it and think, *"Wow, that hurt them so badly."* I would hear *hurt* even though they were using very angry words. Before, I would have reacted to the angry words by asking, "And then what did you do?" Or, "You should have turned the guy in." Instead it was breaking my heart to hear them tell about it. I fell in love with people who had irritated me before or who seemed impossible to understand.

A verse from this same song goes like this *"I know why you're crying, and I know why you're sad. I have come to sit by you, so you don't feel bad."* I traveled all over Orange County and Los Angeles County to talk to students or groups about communication and the game. I would play this song and people would cry.

Two years after I started singing the song at every program, I sang it at Huntington Beach. A man came up afterwards and said, "I know where you got that song because I was transferred here from San Diego School District and they play that at all our meetings." I meekly replied, "Well, I wrote it." From the look on his face, I think he thought I was pulling his leg.

I found out later that someone in the San Diego School District had taped it when I was there. Later, they made a film about volunteerism in the schools with the intent to get parents to volunteer in the classrooms – and *listen*. They used this song in the background of their movie which was circulated all over San Diego. I was totally unaware of this. I eventually got to see their slide presentation which had the most beautiful pictures of parents and kids – with only my song playing in the background.

Through the playing of the game, I also began to feel connected to people for the first time in my life. Since I was a child, I'd felt strange, out of place. Sometimes I felt weird, other times I felt that everyone else was weird. Through the Ungame® sharing process, I found out I was not that different. Other people had pain and hurt and embarrassment and got angry about the same things I did, and they were afraid of things that I was afraid of, but I had never heard anybody talk about them.

So feeling connected was incredible to me. It was like I was finally recognized as part of the human race. I learned in this experience that, in some ways, we are all alike. It was also during this time that I learned to cry. I didn't know tears were okay. I didn't know that people would still consider you to be a together person if you cried. I thought crying meant that you had no faith in God and that you couldn't handle life.

Through the game, I experienced a lot of crying. People would be sitting around the table, weeping. Teachers, business executives, psychologists – whoever I was with – would share a story and then they'd get out tissues or a hanky and start wiping away the tears. We'd all be wiping. I witnessed councilmen breaking down around the game table. At one time, I would have thought, "Wow… and we still voted him in." It was in no way a negative, instead it made me like them better. Then when I shared some of my sad experiences, and people wept with me rather than think less of me, it seemed to bring us closer together. To me, this was a stark revelation. They liked me better knowing how weak I really was.

This was a wonderful connection. I learned that tears were vital, healthy, and healing and certainly nothing to be ashamed of. Years later I became aware of the scientific discoveries regarding tears; those of sadness and grief have a different chemical composition than those from peeling an onion and if not released, they poison the body. They're toxic.

Through these experiences, I found that if I expressed my feelings I stayed healthy. This was of great importance for me. I didn't have the throat trouble that had shadowed me for twenty years. I found out that my history of throat problems was due to bottling up my feelings. This connection came to me one day when I was doodling and pondering the question, *Why am I staying healthy?*

Then an image came to me, a little leather drawstring bag, like my brothers used to keep their marbles in. At first, I didn't understand the implications of this image. Why would a picture of a drawstring pouch – full of marbles – be coming to me forty years later? In my mind, I could see the two strings pulled tight and the neck totally constricted.

Suddenly, I knew that this was me. Now I had to identify with the little strings. I asked myself, what is it that causes my throat to tighten up like that?

The answers came immediately. One was *guilt*! All those years of thinking I was not a good person. All those years of keeping things inside of me, because no one really knew me, nobody seemed to understand. I had felt ashamed and guilty. The other was *resentment* because nobody listened, nobody cared. People were stupid.

Guilt and resentment were killing me. I've discovered they are two sides of the same coin. If you feel guilt, you also feel resentment. It became crystal clear to me that the body is really connected to our thoughts and our feelings. I had never heard that before. So, I made a commitment to find a variety of ways to express my feelings.

I came up with twenty-two ways to express my feelings. Subsequently, I designed a workshop around these different modes. I found that if not given an outlet, energy builds up. This energy finds some sort of expression, some way to start the flow and move out of the body. I *had* to find a way to get the energy to move through me because I could get ticked about so many things. This was vital for my health.

Of the twenty-two ideas I came up with, I think *sharing from the heart* is the most important. Others include writing, painting, drawing, sculpting, running, dancing, singing, working with clay, even washing my car. ***Express, don't depress!***

Keeping feelings bottled up is a detriment to health and well-being. Often, when things upset us, we think we need to deal with the perpetrator directly. I found the opposite is true. I could be mad at Dan for something he did, and instead of taking it out on Dan, I can go out and wash the car. Whoosh, the energy is moved.

160

It doesn't have to be directly connected to the event. Energy is energy.

That was quite a revelation for me. Sometimes you have to deal with the person directly, but if you keep the feelings flowing, you usually don't have to go back to the person and fight it out. You can go feed the homeless and poof... the tension is gone.

Another important principle I ascribe to is *show your love*. The Ungame® relies on a lot of words, but actions are often much more important. One evening, I played the game with Molly, her husband and two children. Molly was in her mid-forties, and I knew that she and her husband were financially well-off. She seemed like a woman who had everything.

Molly drew a card that asked her to talk about a hurtful moment. She answered rather sadly, "When I was six, my mother told me I was too old to be kissed. I felt so bad that every morning I went into the bathroom and looked for the tissue on which she'd blotted her lipstick. I carried it with me all day. Whenever I wanted a kiss, I rubbed the smear of lipstick on my cheek."

This was the first time she had ever revealed this to her family. Molly's life had not been as idyllic as I thought. For almost forty years, she had endured this small, private heartache. *"Can anyone ever make up for that?"* I wondered.

Several turns later, Molly's eight-year-old son landed on a comment space. Quietly, he got up and walked over to his mother. Without a word, he put his thin arms around her neck and kissed her on the cheek. Molly's eyes filled with tears. The old hurt was gone – perhaps for good.

Until I invented the Ungame®, I don't think I ever hugged. Sometimes it seems that I had hardly ever touched another person. I was just not a touchy-feely person. I eventually learned that this was from woundedness. My non-touching era ended during my mute period, when I would hear someone's heart-wrenching story and I would care so much and not be able to say, "Don't worry, it's going to be OK," or "Why don't you go hear this lecture that might help you." I soon learned that a simple, heart-felt touch was much more powerful than all the words I could dream up. And sometimes it takes much more than a simple touch.

~

Many years ago, a pastor friend of mine asked if I would meet with a woman named Christine. She was in her mid-thirties, but she looked like she was twelve. She was very small – less than five feet tall and was a frail little thing. She couldn't have weighed more than seventy-five pounds.

The pastor had gone back to the office late one night for a last minute task and found her there near the church. What choice did he have – it was Christmas Eve. He couldn't just lock up the church and say, "Call me in the morning."

So he took her home and she stayed with the pastor and his wife. Christine had a tragic history. She had tried to take her life several times and had undergone psychiatric care but nothing seemed to work. She was a very troubled person. The pastor and his wife couldn't give her the time that they felt was needed.

So, she came to me. It was almost like she was transparent – she had white hair and pale, pink skin. She was like a ghost with no soul. I remember thinking later that it was as though somebody literally vacuumed out her soul. She was vacant, no feeling, no emotions. Nothing.

I remember sitting on a swing on our patio with this skinny woman. She was like a child, her feet didn't touch the floor, and she sat as far away from me as she possibly could. It was apparent that she didn't feel comfortable sitting very close.

I started asking her questions about her troubled life. She was an only child, and she never made friends. She got excellent grades in school, in fact she had a very high I.Q. She was a genius. In third grade she could do high school work, but she had such emotional problems that they put her in special education classes.

At some point I said, "Christine, I need to get to know you, so why don't you tell me about your childhood."

She sighed, "I've talked about my childhood to every psychiatrist I have ever gone to. They can't find anything wrong with my childhood. It was fine."

I asked her what "fine" was.

She answered as if she'd been over this hundreds of times before. "I had a mother and a father. I was an only child. When I was little my parents took me everywhere. They doted on me. As I got older, they gave me lessons in everything I was interested in – especially dancing and piano. So, as a young child I got applause and standing ovations for my performances. I had a lot of affirmation. There was nothing wrong with my childhood."

We went on and I asked her some other things, but I kept wanting to come back to her childhood. Finally I said, "Would you be willing to close your eyes and take me with you back to your childhood. I want to see what you experienced."

She was okay with that, so I said a prayer and said, "Let's go back to a time when you were very young." I asked her to take me on a tour through her house. I had never heard of anybody doing this but it seemed like a good idea and I felt prompted by the Spirit to do it this way.

She described her house when she was three years old. I asked her where her dad was. "He's in the living room reading the paper."

"Can you go to your dad?"

She said yes, so when she came close to him, I asked her what he does. She said, "He drops the newspaper and picks me up and holds me."

That sounded good to me so I asked her where her mother was. "She's in the kitchen cooking, where she always is."

"Can you go to your mother?"

"Yes." Christine goes to her mother, who puts down her dish towel, picks Christine up and holds her.

At this point I am thinking that this certainly seems like a nice loving family, but then it occurred to me to say, "I don't know why, but go back to your dad again." Again, her father picks her up and holds her. Then I said, "Christine, what is the little girl feeling?"

She was quiet for the longest time. I think she had an extremely difficult time getting in touch with her feelings. But here she was, talking to me as though she was this little girl, and then I said, "What are you feeling while your daddy holds you?" All of a sudden she lets out a scream and doubles over, crying "Oh no – no – no – noooooo!"

I couldn't touch her – she didn't want me to – but I asked her what was happening. She moaned, "He's not *giving* me love, he's *taking* love from me." Again, she let out a loud scream.

So I said, "The little girl can get down out of his lap and go to her mother." She did, and then she said, "She is taking love from me, too!"

I had never heard of anything like this. I didn't understand it, and all I knew was that she wanted out of there. I said, "Can you go to your bedroom?" She said she could, so I asked her to go in there and close the door. She went to her room and sat on the bed, but she was so lonely. She described how she was sitting there, afraid and alone, as I looked at her on the end of our swing, a frail little waif all tensed in a ball.

Finally I said, "Christine, do you believe in Jesus?" She nodded. "Well, he says he is with us always."

"Can you see him somewhere in the room?"

After a long lapse filled with tense silence, Christine says that she sees Jesus. "What is he doing?"

"He is just standing there, looking at me."

"Do you think he wants to say something?"

"He is waiting to see what I want."

"What do you want?"

She says, "I want him to sit with me."

"Can you ask him?"

So this fragile troubled woman (now a three-year-old in her mind's eye) asks Jesus to sit on the bed next to her. I let that happen for a long time, and then I ask if he is saying anything. He isn't doing anything, just sitting with Christine. "How is the little girl feeling?"

"Safe."

"Is he touching you?"

"No."

164

I thought, *"Well of course, Jesus would know she doesn't want to be touched."*

Christine felt safe.

After she came out of the meditation, we talked about what had happened. She had told the psychiatrists, and me, that her parents really loved her, but in the meditation it felt like they were *taking* it from her rather than *giving* it to her. I told her I had never heard of this before.

She said, "I've never been able to love anybody because to me love meant... something that was taken from me. That's why I've never found help in church because they talk about how God loves you and it makes me want to run." In her orientation, love was something that was sucked out of you.

I spent a lot of time thinking about Christine's situation. Her parents had a baby so that someone would love *them*. This left her feeling empty. She was thirty-five, she had never experienced a love relationship, she never had a close friend. This made sense to me, but how do we change it?

A few days later, we met again in the same place on the swing. I asked Christine if I could sit a little closer to her this time. She said, "Well, okay." So I moved over a bit and then I asked her if I could touch her on her shoulder closest to me. She said it would be okay, so I did. She was like a frightened little bird. I don't remember all that we talked about, but I do remember at some point trying to explain to her that real love was something that would flow *into* her, that God's love and another person's love for her would not take anything from her. I told her that I didn't want anything from her. I didn't need her to love me, but I loved her, I cared for her. As I was talking, I was able to slide my arm on the back of the swing over a little more, so that my hand was on her other shoulder and my arm was across her back.

At some point she leaned over in my lap, drew her legs up like a fetus and began to cry. I felt like I had her permission, so I wrapped my arms around this poor little bundle of emotions.

We stayed in this position and swung on the swing for six-and-a-half hours. Christine fell asleep for what seemed like an eternity. I didn't know how to end our time. From the patio, I could see into the kitchen. Dan came home from his job at five o'clock. Christine and I had been together since noon. I saw him peek out at us, then the refrigerator door opened. *Okay, he will get dinner for himself. He sees I'm busy.*

We continued to sit there. It started to get dark, but I didn't feel that I could be the one to initiate ending it. I wasn't always thinking loving thoughts, I wasn't always praying, but every so often I would just say inside myself, *"Love her, Lord, love her, just love her."* I didn't know what else to say.

I was loving her but this was a person who had put up a thick wall. She told me later that she realized how when she was little she made some kind of inner vow to never let anyone love her again, because it took everything from her. Since then she was living in this capsule, starving inside for love, holding on for dear life to what she had. She didn't know that love could come in from others to fill her up.

While she was sleeping, I remember yearning that somehow or other, she would be healed. And I believe I felt when it happened. It felt like when you push and push on something and all of a sudden it gives way. I was swinging with her, loving her and poof... it all let go! Something was different. Over six hours of one feeling and then something changed. Shortly after it happened, Christine opened her eyes, sat up and said, "Oh my gosh, have I kept you?" (She was always very conscious of not taking advantage of others.)

When we stood up, she threw her arms around me. She said, "Thank you, thank you, thank you." We didn't talk about what had happened. She asked if we could talk again the following week. I said sure, as she ran out of the house. The next week she was a different person.

After that, Christine returned to school and graduated with several degrees. She is an absolute genius, and now she is whole inside. She has friends, a good job and enjoys interacting with people, something she was never able to do before.

This experience with Christine (and many since) has helped me understand people who have addictions or compulsions. They are absolutely desperate to get some healing balm into some little place that love hasn't gotten to, and it really isn't hard to get to it. It just takes time and love.

I've come to realize that there are a lot of people around us living with this condition and no one knows it. They think that love is something taken from them so they close up. They know they need something but they don't know what it is, so they go from relationship to relationship, to drinking or drugs, and nothing works. They're looking for love in all the wrong places. Something very important got reversed in their early years, and they didn't receive the love they needed as children.

Chapter 25

My Dream Job

I spent years planning workshops and retreats and constantly learning how to create a place where the Holy Spirit was welcome and could do His work. But since I responded to invitations, I was often in an unfamiliar setting, given a time slot within someone else's time frame. This was good training for me because I had to remain flexible and open to the Spirit. The best plan can fall apart if a fire alarm goes off, or someone faints, or the bathroom floods, or a group meeting in the next room breaks into "Row, row, row your boat," while you are leading a guided meditation about Jesus walking on the water! I remember a church group that wanted to meet in a lovely lodge for a Saturday retreat. They were told they could use the bar room since it didn't open until evening. We were assured it would be quiet. What we weren't told was that above the bar was a life-size nude picture of Burt Reynolds. It was very difficult to keep the attention on the subject of our inner child.

Another time, when meeting in a beautiful campground, there was a fire in one of the cabins during my teaching session. We had to evacuate the camp. This kind of interruption in a plan became practice for living life. God was teaching me to roll with the punches and come to realize that my 'job' wasn't to accomplish something, but rather to model a way of living no matter what is going on. Since what mattered to me was that those in my presence would get to know Jesus, my challenge was to always do what I thought Jesus would do and say what I thought he would say in those situations. I really learned to trust God and never even try to guess what He might accomplish through some experience or message I would share.

~

Dan and I remained members of the United Methodist church I walked into as one who knew nothing about religion sixty years

169

ago. (I never stepped foot inside a church until I was twenty-four years old.) We didn't stay because we were always happy there. I think Dan stayed because it was "the thing we did on Sunday," but I stayed because of a promise I made years ago, and that was to ask God at the beginning of each new year where he wanted me to worship. It always amazed me how the clear signs came to keep me there. I didn't question it during the year. Well, I may have questioned it, but I lived out my promise even though I felt like a voice crying in the wilderness most of the time. I was always on two or three committees and would go home feeling frustrated after most meetings because the group would vote to use endowment money to stripe the parking lot rather than feed the homeless across the street. Or they'd discuss whether to use glass or plastic cups for communion rather than talk about why attendance was declining every year.

I started an early Sunday morning adult class to see if anyone else wanted to talk about spiritual things. It grew to around twenty-four men and women who became faithful attendees. We shared our "God sightings" and had wonderful discussions each week. But I was scolded by one of the pastors when it was noticed that several of those who came to the class no longer attended the worship service. So we decided to meet on a weekday at six A.M. in a local coffee shop, so we didn't feel we were competing with the church's efforts. We met for fifteen years. Some never returned to the church.

Remaining faithful to my commitment in the church was like swimming upstream or being a thorn in their flesh, because I would see visions or have dreams of what this church could become but had little success in finding openness. I became popular in other churches, but not my own. I eventually became District Director of Spiritual Life for forty United Methodist churches and led many retreats for their members, but never for my own church. I don't think I was ever forgiven for taking a group of women to the inner city, which meant they no longer were available to teach Sunday school or cook in the kitchen.

However, in the forty-three years, there were occasional associate pastors who became close friends and co-conspirators for Christ. I could share my dreams and ideas with them, but often did not have the support of the long-time members on the board or the committees in my own church.

At the end of the 43rd year, an interesting thing happened that had never happened before. I completed a four-year-term on a committee with the bishop of the United Methodist Churches in Southern California, my six years as Director of Spiritual Life for the district, and a three-year-term on the local church's Worship Committee *all at the same time.* It was the first time in all those years that I held no position and wasn't asked to serve in any capacity. I knew in my spirit that I was now free to go. But where would I go?

I was often invited to teach and lead classes for other churches and denominations. I led inner healing classes for years at the Crystal Cathedral in Garden Grove, California, in the early 1980's and spoke at their International Women's Conference and the Care & Kindness Conferences almost every year for twenty years. It was there in an interview on their internationally televised *Hour of Power* with Dr. Robert H. Schuller that the Ungame® gained popularity around the world. So I was better known at that church than in my own. And it was at the Crystal Cathedral where I found my "next assignment." I was asked by the director of women's ministries to assume the leadership of a group of older women that had met for fifty years, but now was declining in numbers.

I was trusted and given permission to design the class of my dreams using all that I had learned. I was so excited, it brought me to my knees. I was being trusted to reshape a group of women who had been together for years. I knew it would be delicate to make any changes, so I prayed that I could meet them where they were and get to know them before trying anything new. I asked the Lord how to begin and felt God saying to begin with a four-week series on the story of Abraham. I was confident they knew the story since they'd been in Bible studies for decades. But the questions I would ask would give them new insights.

Everyone sat in her 'reserved' seat and we sang their hymns with ninety-year-old Norma at the piano. I learned about the ladies from their prayer requests and from observing them, and it was obvious they were not used to interaction. They waited for me to answer my own questions. I learned they weren't used to laughing in a Bible study either. But it was clear to me that they were dear Saints who loved the Lord.

However, I could tell they were comfortable with their way of doing things, so I went slowly, trying to stay tuned in to what Jesus would do. I was challenged to see if we could turn up the Light in this group (with an average age of 78) to a brightness that would draw women of all ages to follow Jesus.

I began to dramatize my Bible lessons, causing the women to think of the old familiar stories in a deeper way. I would have them turn to their neighbor and talk about what they learned (which was new to them). Music was always an important part of my ministry. I would choose songs that would reinforce the message I wanted to communicate. For years I had played my guitar and led singing at camps and retreats, but I heard some murmuring in the group about not liking "contemporary music." I prayed about how to introduce guitar music so I could interject a chorus in my message without having to call Norma up to the piano to find it in the song book. I felt led to ask, "Who remembers going to camp when you were young?" Almost everyone raised her hand. When I asked if they remembered any songs from those days, they began to call out songs like *Kum ba ya, Jacob's Ladder, Do Lord, and I've Got the Joy, Joy, Joy.* I picked up my guitar and started strumming and they were delighted to sing along. From then on I was able to slowly introduce praise choruses and contemporary hymns. The group began to loosen up. They clapped their hands, smiled, and sang with gusto. I even taught them some hand motions and opened my suitcase of rhythm instruments so they would play along.

It was as though I was fanning a flickering flame that began to grow and glow more brightly. There was new energy in the room. I never knew how the word spread, but women began to show up. It had to be the Lord.

The chairs had always been in eight straight rows like a classroom. A new person would always sit in the back row where all they could see was the backs of heads. (Not a very welcoming arrangement.) I was told that some ladies were upset if the chairs were arranged differently by a group using the room before them. When I talked to the Lord about that, I was reminded of why I'd been teaching on Abraham. So I had a lesson about how difficult it must have been for Abraham and his family to pack up everything and leave their land without knowing where God was calling them. Since I want all of my lessons to involve experiencing some part of the story, I challenged them to imagine God telling us to leave our comfortable surroundings and go to someplace new. For our experiment, I proposed that during a break, I would rearrange the chairs in a horseshoe shape, and that each lady would choose a different seat, so we could experience our willingness to be "moveable." It worked! There were giggles as they 'shopped' for the right seat in the new configuration. The chairs remained that way from then on, but each week we had to add a few more chairs because more women were coming to join us.

After four or five weekly meetings (which I extended to two hours rather than the usual ninety minutes), I selected eight women to train to be small group leaders. We had an all-day session where we talked about the principles of a meaningful sharing experience. I created a "tower" to set in the center of each group's table that listed the group guidelines, as reminders.

173

1. LISTEN: Give others your full attention.
2. NO ADVICE: We are not here to "fix" each other.
                       God will do the fixing.
3. BE FAIR: Let everyone have time to share.
4. BE TRUSTWORTHY: Keep sharing confidential.
5. STAY ON TOPIC: Save other topics for after class.

From that time on, the women were assigned to a small group for one year where they spent time together during Bible study. Then they were put in a new group for the next year. Everyone prayed that God would direct the assigning and agreed not to question it, but rather go with a sense of excitement and wonder about the new mix of women God wanted them to journey with. This eliminated the cliques that often form in groups and created a sense of community as we became acquainted with the others. We chose the name: Women of the Word, or WOW! We were women practicing living in the Kingdom.

I taught the groups the difference between what I call Head Talk and Heart Talk, which are two very different languages. Knowing the difference and being able to identify another's language, makes all the difference in the world if you want to communicate. If you want to connect with another person, speak the same language. Otherwise there can be miscommunication, leaving one person feeling misunderstood and disconnected. In our small groups we spoke Heart Talk. Healing happened and love flowed.

Of course, I always needed to choose Bible stories to prepare the ladies for each change I made in their familiar routine. I relied on the Holy Spirit as I prepared 450 new lessons, one for each week for the next eight years. It was an exciting challenge and a deeply spiritual experience. We left our Bibles at home, had no workbooks or homework. But we were changed because we were not just talking about the Word, we were working out the Word. We were *doing it.* We changed our name to the Women's WorkOut.

Each week I had an activity to move our learning from head to heart to bones. We danced, expressed ourselves through art and clay, and created centerpieces to symbolize our lives.

We experimented with different prayer postures and role-played Bible characters. We made prayer bracelets and prayer shawls. We packed Blessing Bags to give to the homeless. All of these activities gave the women something to share during the week and they were changed. They became bold in their faith and witness by their actions.

After years of speaking on communication, then healing, I now focus on prayer. I want to help people discover the many ways God might speak to them. I believe God is always speaking. I don't think he goes to a switchboard when someone prays and responds just to them. I've come to believe that the Omnipresent God is always shouting, offering everything we need to know before we ask, but we don't take the time to listen… or don't really want to know what God would have us do. After all, we might have an appointment to get our hair or nails done! Or we're tired or scared. After reviewing the many ways God spoke in the Bible (burning bush, rainbows, manna, audible voice, angels, parables, and even a donkey!), I created exercises to teach us how to tune in and hear God give personal messages. We found nearly fifty ways

God might be speaking to us if we had ears to hear and eyes to see. Our prayers become dialogues rather than monologues.

What's at the Heart of Comm U N I cation ?

Head Talk (Can divide people)	Heart Talk (Will unite people)
Expressing opinions	Sharing thoughts
Imparting information	Bringing inspiration
Stating theories	Offering ideas
Asking questions	Sharing 'wonderings'
Quoting facts	Expressing feelings
Preaching	Sharing experiences
Trying to influence	Accepting one another
Proving a point	Showing concern
Trying to "solve"	Trying to "salve"
Critiquing others	Affirming others
Talking re: tangibles (cars, broken bones, real estate)	Talk re: intangibles (cares, broken hearts, relationships)
Head Talk Is for DEALING	Heart Talk is for HEALING

Rhea Zakich @ copyright 1998

We carried bookmarks to remind us of some of the ways God might speak.

Scripture, Nature, Sky, Sunsets, Music, Dreams, Pain, Suffering, Books, Poetry, People, Children, Change, Imagination, Ministers, Teachers, Ideas, Thoughts, Meditation, Silence, Intuition, Hunches, Nudges, Promptings, Feelings, Emotions, Relationships, Miracles, Parables, Fairy Tales, Pets, Humor, Events, Circumstances, Opportunities, Birth, Death, Physical Body, History, Seasons, Provision, Art, Writing, Connections, Angels, Desires, Liturgy, Sacraments, Mistakes, Touch, and Coincidences

Almost every week someone would share a story of hearing from God in one of these ways. This created a spirit of expectancy and attentiveness.

One time I asked each of the twelve small groups to design and build a worship station for an Hour of Prayer, using their member's creativity and items. They each selected a theme and secretly worked together for two weeks. It was a day I'll never forget, when one hundred women moved as the Spirit led them from one station to another in absolute silence for a full hour. They moved as the Spirit led, praying in many ways: writing prayers at a prayer wall, nailing burdens to a cross, burning confessions, washing hands and feet, being anointed with oil, and receiving prayers for healing. They received communion and lit candles as they prayed for others. Not a word was spoken for one hour.

These are some of the notes I received afterward.

Rhea, I have never, in all my years, experienced anything like our day of prayer. I was in tears the entire time. I still feel the

covering, a day later. I do believe it is the longest I have ever been silent before the Lord. Doris C.

Yesterday was and is, and always will be a blessing in my memory. I felt the presence of the Holy Spirit in all that happened - the touches, the music, the eye contact, the anointing, and crumpling my sins and tossing them in the trash, You are a treasure! Thanks, Anne W.

When I came today, I was overwhelmed with grief over my husband's recent death. By the time I sat at the various stations I began to be thankful for all the happy years we had. Shirley A.

Dear Rhea, Thanks for your direct line to God and all the good things He provides to us through you. We are all so blessed by your love and dedication to WOW. I was so touched by the presence of the Holy Spirit and how it touched so many. I was overwhelmed by the hugs, love, and the whole experience. What an awesome God we honor with our obedience. Mary G.

In my 51 years as a Christian, I've never experienced anything like our time together. It was magnificent. Clara L.

Thank you, Rhea, for your foresight in making this a wonderful day for us women of WOW. It was a special day with Jesus. It was overwhelming, unbelievable, and beautiful. My faith is stronger. God bless you. Dorothy G.

The Hand of the Lord was on you, Rhea. The day was awesome... a mountain top experience. Each station spoke volumes to me. Tears flowed freely... I felt Jesus... close... talking with me. It was a "Sweet Hour of Prayer." Trudi A.

Dear Rhea, The day was amazing! You could feel the presence of the Holy Spirit leading. It was a very moving experience - we were all blessed. My husband couldn't believe that there were all those women together and no one spoke for an hour! Judi L.

I am humbled and overwhelmed with joy as I reflect on that day and experience. For many long-time Christians, it was the first time they'd ever *experienced* the presence of the Living God. I give all glory to God for His faithfulness. There's no way the day would have had the life-changing results had the Spirit of our Loving Lord not been present. We tasted Kingdom living.

It was a perfect day. I was able to use all that I had been learning over the years. How blessed I was to be able to design every part of it: the room arrangement, the lighting, the visuals and sounds, and the timing, all to unite a very diverse group of women and help them open their entire being to the Holy Spirit.

Every lesson I taught was based on what we experienced the week before. I had gained the trust and confidence of the women so they were willing to follow the plan and instructions. I never felt I would be good at evangelism, but I have learned how to bring people to Jesus by making them hungry and thirsty, then walking with them. God has shown me how to set people free. The Holy Spirit is waiting for us to be open and available for His wisdom and power. When we are, heaven only knows what we will find.

Chapter 26

Still Enjoying the Journey

I no longer ask, *"Is this all there is?"* since I now know there is *so* much more. In some ways, at age 84, I feel as though I've just begun. I still want to learn and experience all that God has for me, so I remain active and involved in life.

In 2012, I was sensing that I should let go of my role as leader of the Women's WorkOut after eight wonderful years. The group was still growing and filled with spiritual vitality, but the Lord showed me there were leaders emerging. Women, who had grown strong in their faith and discovered their spiritual gifts, were now offering to assist in many ways. When I finally announced my retirement as their leader, five women quickly assumed the responsibilities of welcoming/announcements, song leader, prayer time, the lesson, handling small group time, and a closing celebration. The group continued almost without missing a step. God was using the new leaders in a mighty way. I did not attend for the next year so the new leaders could gain respect and trust. I felt my presence would shift the focus, so to honor them, I stayed away. I really missed "my women."

That same year, Dan and I decided (after living in our Garden Grove home for fifty years) to move to Town & Country Manor, a Christian-based retirement center with three levels of care, to prepare for the days ahead. We both liked to plan ahead since we learned that we'd rather choose to let go of something we love before we have to, rather than try to hold on to it until something happens and our choices are taken away. Many of our friends waited too long and had a bad fall, a stroke, a heart attack, or an ailment that required a caregiver. We wanted to make the move while we could still enjoy the adventure of a whole new lifestyle. So at ages of 77 and 84, we sold or gave away almost everything we owned except what would fit in a two-room apartment. We started a new adventure. It was indeed different being part of a community of people we didn't choose as friends, but it was the right move for us. We participated in various activities and attended programs and concerts that were offered there.

Our 60th wedding anniversary celebration.

Then Dan began to lose interest in things, and he slept more. Eventually, he was diagnosed with Alzheimer's and for the next two years, life seemed to proceed in slow motion. I went through the disease with him, as did our wonderful and supportive sons, Darin and Dean, who faithfully came every Saturday to spend time with their dad. They wanted to give me a break since my life was on hold and Dan's condition was worsening. But instead of going somewhere when they came, we used the time for family conversation and reflection. We would answer Ungame® questions and laugh as we recalled things we did as a family. This enabled us to watch the decline in Dan's ability to think clearly or speak coherently.

Dan died peacefully in 2019, with us by his side. We all felt up to date with everything being said and done that needed to be said and done. We'd had 61 years together: a full life. What more could we ask? Having made so many wonderful friends in our seven years at the retirement center, I was surrounded by people with compassion and support as I went through his memorial service and the paperwork. That was a blessing.

Darin and Dean continue to spend time with me. We take hikes, go to plays and concerts, check out new restaurants, and really enjoy just hanging out together. Dean is happy being single. Darin and Maria gave us two beautiful granddaughters that we got to watch grow up at the many family get-togethers in our home. I am blessed to have all four of my siblings living and I enjoy being with them. Yes, life is good. Thanks be to God.

Enjoying my boys, Darin and Dean.

What is my purpose now?

This new part of my journey has become one of finding ways to weave the diverse men and women residents in this community into a tapestry of love and caring by helping them find connections. They come from different places with different backgrounds, but they all have a story to tell, and they've all left what was familiar and they want to fit in.

I asked God how to do such a thing when I was the "new kid on the block." He gave me an immediate thought (so I knew it wasn't mine) to volunteer to be the editor of the monthly paper for the Manor. *"But Lord, I've never done that before."* I think I heard God laugh. *He* knows that *I* know that knowing how to do something has nothing to do with whether or not I report for duty. When I say yes to things I don't know how to do, God will work through me, and I'll know it's him and not me that brings the results.

My favorite way to draw stories out of people is still to play the Ungame®. So we have a weekly Ungame® Night when we discover all sorts of interesting things about our new neighbors. What a difference this has made with people finding they have something in common with someone else, like both coming from Chicago, or serving in the military, or being a violinist or a dancer. Or maybe it's that they enjoy playing Bridge or golf, or enjoy sewing, or gardening. Our community is a loving, caring group of friendly men and women.

Every day God leads me to certain people to interview so they can tell a longer version of their story. I then take their picture and feature them in the *Manor Mirror*, along with devotional articles, stories about missionaries, and reports.

I am excited to get up every morning because I know that God has something planned for me. I'm even part of a ukulele band that leads sing-alongs in assisted living and skilled nursing. I'm active in a Spirit-filled church and speak to various groups and classes there. The church is my filling station and wherever I am is my mission field. I walk and talk with God throughout the day. I have been richly blessed and love being a blessing to others.

Our group, Rod & the UkuLadies, playing and singing for residents.

I have a tremendous sense of peace and am able to let go of negative thoughts that creep into my mind. I feel such love for all people. I weep when I see the homeless and grieve for those who make terrible mistakes and are in jails and prisons. Jesus knows how to heal the wounds that caused them to do a bad thing. I'm sad for those who have been abused and I'm sad for the abusers. We who call ourselves by his name should be healers rather than people who judge.

Help us, Jesus.

Acknowledgements

As I look back at my tracks and stepping stones for 84 years of my life, certain people stand out in my memory as very important in my journey.

Mr. Bracken, the first African American teacher in my Ohio high school, changed my learned prejudice into acceptance of people with different skin color.

Rev. Jim Stewart, the pastor who led my first Bible study and encouraged me to believe and trust God.

Peace Pilgrim, a woman who gave up everything, trusting God to supply all her needs as she walked more than 25,000 miles speaking on peace of mind and world peace. She taught me to trust.

Helen Line, who came into my life when I needed something to offer the people in the inner city. She taught Laubach Literacy and equipped me to teach others to read.

Glenn Clark, the man who founded Camps Farthest Out, week-long retreats where I could experience the presence of God and Kingdom Living in profound ways.

Betts Rivet, who believed in my handmade communication game, took my hand and led me to a printer who turned my dream into something tangible.

Lew Herndon, who ignored the 26 rejections I'd had and invested his life in creating the Ungame® Company to launch its success around the world. He believed in me.

Erline Krebs, the teacher who asked her students to interview someone whose story was in the local newspaper. After being taken to her class, she became a connector with other teachers and professors.

Elaine Haglund, the college professor who invited me to her classes to demonstrate how the Ungame® could teach communication skills and help players gain understanding. She gave me teaching experience.

Kitty Paladin, who created my first professional brochure to announce my availability to speak to groups, resulting in an average of 26 speaking engagements a year for many years. This gave me confidence and exposure to a wide variety of people and groups.

Michelle Cavinder who trusted me to redesign and lead a women's Bible study with a long history. Her confidence, support and prayers provided the wind beneath my wings. Together, with God's help, we witnessed the group growing from 30 to 125 women during our eight years together. This experience was the fulfillment of a dream for me.

Janet Elliott, a writer who offered to help me write this book (almost insisted). I couldn't have done it without her constant encouragement, willingness, and dedication to spend the time putting my words in a form that makes sense.

Author

Rhea currently lives in a retirement center in Santa Ana, California and continues to lead weekly classes on a variety of topics such as prayer, healing, and dreams. She also writes the monthly newsletter, the *Manor Mirror*, for her community which gives her opportunities to meet and connect with other residents. She continues to play the Ungame® with her friends and neighbors. Rhea never stops learning, leading, and connecting. It was fifty years ago that God gave me the idea. What a miracle!

Rhea can be contacted at rheazakich@aol.com. You can also visit her website at www.rheazakich.com. The Ungame® has now passed five-million in sales and can be purchased at Amazon.com.